THE PETROS PROPHECY

SIMON PETER'S PROPHETIC WARNING ABOUT THE HERESY OF THE LAST DAYS

By Dr. Scott Lively

*The Petros Prophecy: Simon Peter's Warning
About The Heresy of the Last Days*
is a publication of The Old Paths Publications Inc.

ISBN 978-0-9987778-8-7

Copyright, Scott Douglas Lively, 2017, All Rights Reserved

Scriptural quotations are from the King James Bible
and the New American Standard Bible.

All proceeds from this book support the ministry of Dr. Scott Lively, missionary to the global pro-family movement. To request a trial subscription to Dr. Lively's monthly newsletter, you may contact him through his website at www.defendthefamily.com
or by mail c/o Abiding Truth Ministries,
PO Box 2373, Springfield, MA 01101.

THE OLD PATHS PUBLICATIONS, Inc.
142 Gold Flume Way
Cleveland, Georgia, U.S.A.
Web: www.theoldpathspublications.com
E-mail: TOP@theoldpathspublications.com

Table of Contents

Prologue: A Brief Summary of "Gay Theology" and its Origins ...... 3.

Introduction: The Biblical Warning of a Last Days Heresy ...... 9.

Chapter One: The Prophecy of Simon Peter ...... 13.

Chapter Two: The Days of Noah ...... 21.

Chapter Three: Sodom and Gomorrah ...... 27.

Chapter Four: Lot's Life Circumstances ...... 39.

Chapter Five: The Way of Balaam ...... 47.

Conclusion: Will the Church Heed the Warning? ...... 55.

Appendix A: The Full Text of Biblical Passages Cited in this Book ...... 61.

Appendix B: Six Prophetic Essays Regarding "Gay Theology" by Dr. Lively: ...... 83.
- A Warning to the Church in America ...... 85.
- Church Warning Update ...... 93.
- A Letter to the International Pro-Family Movement ...99.
- The (Potentially) Bright Future of the Pro-Family Movement ...... 109.
- "Gay Pride" and the Wrath of God ...... 115.
- "Gay" Recovery, Recidivism and Grace ...... 119.

End Notes ...... 125.
About the Author ...... 127.

THE PETROS PROPHECY: SIMON PETER'S WARNING ABOUT THE HERESY OF THE LAST DAYS

Prologue:

A BRIEF SUMMARY OF "GAY THEOLOGY" AND ITS ORIGINS

In 1991, in the early days of my ministry, my family took in an ex-"gay" man named Sonny Weaver who was dying of AIDS. My wife and I cared for him in our home for the last year of his life (he died in '92). Formerly the manager of a "gay" apartment complex, Sonny lost both his job and his home when he converted to Christ. His "gay" friends would not tolerate his choice to leave the homosexual lifestyle and, despite his debilitating medical issues, threw him out on the street to fend for himself.

A few days later we met him at church, heard his predicament, and invited him to live with us. We became close friends over the next year, and Sonny helped me to understand the inner workings of the LGBT movement at a time when I was still learning my role as the State Communications Director for the (anti-homosexuality) No Special Rights Act in Oregon (aka Ballot Measure 9).

Sonny had been a "gay" activist for many years and knew many of the leaders of the movement, some intimately. Among those leaders was Troy Perry, the founder of the first homosexual "church" network, known today as the Universal Fellowship of Metropolitan Community Churches.

Sonny told me that his relationship with "Reverend" Perry included a cocaine-fueled "gay" orgy and hot tub party. To be clear, while I believed him, I have no proof and am not repeating this to insist this event actually occurred. My point is that IF it occurred it would be LESS an offense to God than the heresy that God condones, even approves, homosexuality itself. Frankly, if the spiritual truth behind unequivocal Biblical statutes like Leviticus 18:22 – *"You shall not lie with a man as with a woman: it is an abomination"* – can be ignored, then ALL sexual morality becomes a matter of personal choice, including "gay" orgies in hot tubs.

My concern, even then, was not Perry's purported antics (we've seen worse by "straight" pastors), but with the fact that a "gay" denomination had formed, claiming to be Christian. This concern launched me on an investigation of so-called "gay theology" that – 25 years later -- has culminated in this book.

Perry may be, in a broad sense, the most important pioneer of "gay theology" in America for having established a homosexual congregation in 1968 in Huntington, California, which grew over time into a large network of "gay churches." His 1972 book *The Lord is My Shepherd and He Knows I'm Gay*, was one of the very first to advance the heretical argument that the Bible condones homosexual sin.

However, Perry was more of a political activist than a theologian, founding the first "Gay Pride" parade in 1970 and taking a hands-on role in such iconic culture war battles as the vicious personal attack on Anita Bryant in 1977. His "church," especially in the early years, appears to have been more a front for political action than a religious entity.

Another person often considered to be the "father" of "gay theology" is John Eastburn Boswell, a history professor at Yale. He published the first of two books advancing a false homosexuality-affirming interpretation of the Bible in 1980: *Christianity, Social Tolerance and Homosexuality.* Boswell later published *The Marriage of Likeness: Same-Sex Unions in Pre-Modern Europe* in 1994 shortly before dying of AIDS that same year at the age of 47.

Boswell's 1980 book was preceded by and based upon an extensive article he published anonymously in the early 1970s. That article (according to McNeill himself) influenced John J. McNeill, an openly homosexual Jesuit priest, who published *The Church and the Homosexual* in 1976.

McNeill's book was a call to normalize homosexuality in Christendom, which he had been facilitating in the Catholic church since 1969 as a pioneer of the intra-church "gay" activist group DignityUSA, of which he founded a New York chapter in 1972.

McNeill was expelled from the Jesuits in 1987 on the order of Pope Benedict (then Cardinal Ratzinger) after (among otherr things) publicly and persistently opposing a Vatican publication reaffirming the Biblical view of homosexual sin: *On the Pastoral Care of Homosexual Persons* (a document well worth reading even by non-Catholics).

The earliest proponent of the "gay theology" heresy as we recognize it today, however, is Derrick Sherwin Bailey who wrote *Homosexuality and the Western Christian Tradition* in 1955. He was the first to advance the notions that Sodom was destroyed not for homosexuality but for "inhospitality," and that it was only homosexual acts by heterosexuals that were condemned in the Bible, while the homosexuality of people with innate homosexual identity is not condemned (the latter concept containing the germ of what would later be called "sexual orientation" theory).

In 1987, the sometimes cleverly crafted but always Biblically fraudulent arguments of Perry, Boswell, McNeill, Bailey and their fellow heretics were appropriated by the larger LGBT movement to open a new battlefront in the then-raging culture war. A highly influential article titled "The Overhauling of Straight America" was published in the November issue of the now defunct "gay" publication *Guide Magazine*. It was the blueprint for a new political strategy that included the following advice:

> When conservative churches condemn gays...we can use talk to muddy the moral waters. This means publicizing support for gays by more moderate churches, raising theological objections of our own about conservative interpretations of biblical

teachings, and exposing hatred and inconsistency. Second, we can undermine the moral authority of homophobic churches by portraying them as antiquated backwaters, badly out of step with the times and with the latest findings of psychology.

Against the mighty pull of institutional Religion one must set the mightier draw of Science & Public Opinion (the shield and sword of that accursed "secular humanism"). Such an unholy alliance has worked well against churches before, on such topics as divorce and abortion."

"Gay Theology" advanced rapidly from that point as a weapon against Biblical Christianity employed by the entire political left. It became a staple of leftist rhetoric in the 1990s, even to the point of being regularly incorporated in classroom lectures across multiple academic disciplines in secular colleges and universities. Now in the new millennium, it is commonplace to hear even high school students – with no knowledge whatsoever of the Bible itself – spouting false "gay theology" talking points such as "Jesus never said spoke against homosexuality."

We will not delineate and debate all the points of "gay theology" in this book. That work has been thoroughly completed by such qualified scholars as Dr. Robert Gagnon in *The Bible and Homosexual Practice: Texts and Hermeneutics* (2001) and Dr. James De Young's

Homosexuality: Contemporary Claims Examined in Light of the Bible and Other Ancient Literature and Law (2000).

Instead, this book will state the Biblical case against homosexuality as a single comprehensive but multi-faceted warning from God, in a way that no prior publication has done.

It is enough to simply summarize that "gay theology" is a doctrine which asserts that the Bible does not actually condemn homosexuality, but affirms it. The condemnation is claimed to be the result of faulty interpretation, and an alternate, pro-homosexual interpretation is offered for each passage in which homosexuality is addressed.

"Gay theology" is easily refuted but as with so many things in the world today, the politically correct view trumps what is actually true in the minds of many. As Paul noted about human society in his commentary on homosexual sin: "*They suppress the truth in unrighteousness*" (Romans 1:18).

As always, however, if you know what the truth is and why it is true, you won't be fooled by lies. My goal is for the readers of this book to have sufficient command of the Bible's actual teaching on homosexuality that the fallacies of "gay theology" will be glaringly obvious – even to those who first encounter them in detail at some point in the future.

Introduction:

THE BIBLICAL WARNING OF A LAST DAYS HERESY

"Now the serpent was more subtle than any beast of the field which the LORD God had made. And he said unto the woman, Yea, has God said, you shall not eat of every tree of the garden?" (Genesis 3:1).

Did God really mean what He said? Is He trying to cheat you out of something good by the restrictions that He placed on you? Can you really trust His Word about anything?

Eve knew full well what God has said, but she learned from the serpent how to rationalize her way to disobedience by casting doubt on God's authority. In that instant she gave birth to heresy, and from that moment all human beings have been susceptible to it.

A heresy in Christianity is a belief or set of beliefs that contradicts the plain truth of scripture to the spiritual peril of those who embrace it. Jude, the brother of Jesus, opened his letter of rebuke of early-church heretics by exhorting the faithful to...

"...Contend earnestly for the faith which was once for all handed down to the saints. For certain persons have crept in unnoticed, those who were long beforehand marked out for their condemnation, ungodly persons who turn the grace of God into licentiousness and deny our only Master and Lord, Jesus Christ" (Jude 1:3-4).

Jude, in his *"desire to remind you"* of what is in contest, invokes *"Sodom and Gomorrah and the cities around them, since they all in the same way as these indulged in gross immorality and went after strange flesh"* and warns *"Yet in the same way these [last days heretics]...defile the flesh, and reject authority...following after their own ungodly lusts. These are the ones who cause divisions, worldly minded, devoid of the Spirit"* (v.8-19).

Now, before we plainly state what is clearly being identified by Jude as the last days heresy, and trigger the avalanche of outrage and denial that always attends this topic, let us remember one other critical prerequisite in our analysis, which is the subtlety of the Father of Lies in the last days. To be the "heresy of the last days" it must be so completely beguiling to those confronted with it that *"if it were possible, even the elect would be deceived."*

We're therefore not looking for gross and blatant fallacies such as the claims of false religions, but sophistry, meaning intricately woven false reasoning. We're looking for very subtle falsehoods, casually being passed off as if they were authentic Christian doctrines, such as:

- **Substituting naive humanistic idealism for Biblical reasoning, thus putting emotionalism above truth.**

- **Redefining Christian love to exclude any moral discernment or judgment, thus equating compassion with condoning sin.**

- **Misrepresenting Jesus Christ to cast Him as a moral reformer at odds with the Father, thus contradicting His own assertion that "*I and the Father are one.*"**

- **Emasculating Jesus to insist He is a passivist incapable of incinerating Sodom or killing His enemies at Armageddon, thus suppressing the truth about His impending role as the Lord of Hosts and Judge of the Earth.**

To be the Satanic heresy of the last days, it must be a form of sophistry so crafty that it makes those who embrace it claim moral superiority over those who actually follow Christ and believe His Word as it is written. And it must be related to sexuality.

There is really only one ideology in Christendom today that fits these criteria: "gay theology."

THE PETROS PROPHECY: SIMON PETER'S WARNING ABOUT THE HERESY OF THE LAST DAYS

Chapter One:

THE PROPHECY OF SIMON PETER

There is perhaps no better authority for exposing and defining the last days heresy than Simon Peter, the acknowledged leader of the early church, called Petros ("a rock") by Jesus. Having served as a stalwart guardian of faith and doctrine for more than thirty years following the ascension of the Lord, he warned in his final message to the church (around 66AD) that the very heresy that had arisen in his time would define the last days as well:

*"[T]here will also be **false teachers among you, who will secretly introduce destructive heresies**, even denying the Master who bought them, bringing swift destruction upon themselves. **Many will follow their sensuality, and because of them the way of the truth will be maligned**...*

*"For if God did not spare...the ancient world, but preserved Noah...when He brought a flood upon the world of the ungodly; and if He condemned the cities of Sodom and Gomorrah to destruction by reducing them to ashes, having made them an example to those who would live ungodly lives thereafter.... And if He rescued righteous Lot, oppressed by the **sensual conduct of unprincipled men***

...then the Lord knows how to rescue the godly from temptation, and to keep the unrighteous under punishment for the day of judgment, especially those who indulge the flesh in its corrupt desires and despise authority...

*"But these, like unreasoning animals, born as creatures of instinct...count it a pleasure to revel in the daytime...reveling in their deception...**having eyes full of adultery that never cease from sin, enticing unstable souls...** [T]hey have gone astray, having followed the way of Balaam.....**speaking out arrogant words of vanity they entice by fleshly desires, by sensuality,** those who barely escape from the ones who live in error, **promising them freedom while they themselves are slaves of corruption;** for by what a man is overcome, by this he is enslaved"* (2 Peter 2:1-19).

Now let us state plainly that to which we alluded above: To support an imposter is to deny the true King. One doesn't need to deny Christ openly to deny Christ, and indeed, the form of denial of Him that leads "Christians" to believe they are affirming Him is in some ways the greater Satanic victory. The "nicer than Jesus" Jesus to whom the heretics pay homage is not "*the Master who bought them*," he is a false Christ.

Next let's recognize that the heresy in question is defined generally by "*sensuality*" or "*fleshly desires*," meaning sexual conduct and the ideology associated with it. Not doctrinal conflicts like predestination vs free will, or Sunday vs Saturday Sabbath. Not moral license generally.

There is nothing here to suggest that the roster of sinners being identified by Peter includes gamblers, thieves, murderers, perjurers or any other group than the sexually corrupt.

So what sexual conduct is at issue, specifically? We're given four bases of reference: 1) the Days of Noah, 2) Sodom and Gomorrah, 3) Lot's Life Circumstances, and 4) the Way of Balaam. As we will show, the specific sexual sins at issue are the very ones condemned by God in Leviticus Chapter 18, the most egregious of which is identified by God as homosexuality. This is the plain truth that "gay theology" was invented to obscure and suppress.

To properly analyze this topic, especially in light of the tremendous controversy it generates, we must examine Peter's four reference points in the context of the larger teaching on sexual sin in the Bible, from Genesis to Revelation.

The "One Flesh" Paradigm.

A paradigm is precise model or sample. The "one flesh" paradigm is God's exclusive model for human sexuality and the sample He used in the Bible as an analogy to explain His relationship with mankind.

In **Genesis 1:27 & 2:24** God set forth the exclusive "one flesh" paradigm for sexuality: the lifelong, faithful union of one man and one woman created in His image for procreation. *"So God created man in his own image, in* *the image of God created he him; male and female created he them"* (1:27). *"Therefore shall a man leave his father and his mother and cleave unto his wife; and they shall become one flesh"* (2:24).

The *"one flesh"* paradigm was expressly reaffirmed by Jesus in Matthew 19:6 and Mark 10:8, a fact that directly contradicts the claim of "gay theology" that Jesus never spoke against homosexuality. To affirm that heterosexual marriage is God's exclusive venue for sexual expression is to firmly reject homosexuality.

This male/female complementarity, exemplified in "one flesh" and consummated in marriage, reflects the very relationship of God and Man, as the Apostle Paul explains in Ephesians 5, citing Genesis 2:24.

"Husbands, love your wives, even as Christ also loved the church, and gave himself for it; That he might sanctify and cleanse it with the washing of water by the word, That he might present it to himself a glorious church, not having spot, or wrinkle, or any such thing; but that it should be holy and without blemish. So ought men to love their wives as their own bodies. He that loveth his wife loveth himself. For no man ever yet hated his own flesh; but nourisheth and cherisheth it, even as the Lord the church: **For we are members of his body, of his flesh, and of his bones. 'For this cause shall a man leave his father and mother, and shall be joined unto his wife, and they two shall be one flesh.' This is a great mystery: but I speak concerning Christ and the church."**

All sex outside of marriage is thus wrong and harmful -- spiritually equivalent to worshiping false gods -- as in fact God condemns as "adultery" all idolatry by His people.[1]

WHY GOD CONDEMNS SEXUAL SIN SO HARSHLY

Sexual sin is specially addressed in the Bible because, as shown above, it defiles both God's image in us and His relationship with us, making it particularly grievous in the eyes of God and specially condemned in scripture.

The teaching of Leviticus 18, which we will address shortly, makes clear God's perspective that sexual sin is the most destructive of all sins to human society and our relationship to Him. It is important to highlight this fact before we proceed to examine the lessons of Genesis 6-19.

As Paul explains *"Every other sin that a man commits is outside the body, but the immoral man sins against his own body. Do you not know that your body is a temple of the Holy Spirit who is in you, whom you have from God, and that you are not your own?"* (1 Corinthians 6:18-19).

Every human body was created to be a temple of the Holy Spirit! Through Christ, the bodies of the elect are cleansed and made inhabitable by Him. But there is more to this teaching than just the fact that illicit sex defiles the temple.

In the Sermon on the Mount Jesus condensed the Ten Commandments of the Mosaic law down to just two: *"You shall love the Lord your God with all your heart, soul, mind and strength"* (1-4) and *"You shall love your neighbor as yourself"* (5-10).

In that same teaching, Jesus highlighted two sins which violate both of the two great commandments simultaneously: murder and adultery. Variations of these two sins -- child sacrifice and sexual perversion – defined the demon worship of the Canaanites and are catalogued in Leviticus 18.

Humans tend to think of genocide as the worst possible sin. But in fact God Himself *employed* genocide (by the Hebrews) as a punishment of the Canaanites for child sacrifice and sexual perversion. In God's perspective (as revealed in Leviticus 18), the worst human sin is violation of the first of the Ten Commandments: *"You shall have no other gods before me"* and Canaanite demon worship was the most egregious example of that rebellion in all of scripture.

Contrary to human moral calculations, God emphasized sexual sin as the more offensive of the two – equating the human choice to indulge in perversion to demon worship in His Holy Temple (such as triggered the Babylonian exile of the Jews as we will discuss below).

Importantly, however, God does not define all sexual sin as equally harmful.

DEVIATION EQUALS CONDEMNATION

Just as in manufacturing, where a product's quality and usefulness is measured by its closeness to a carefully prepared design, human sexual conduct is judged based on its closeness to the Creator's *"one flesh"* design.

What we see in scripture is the further that sexual relationships deviate from the model of faithful, marriage-based heterosexual monogamy, the more harshly they are condemned. Thus, moderate heterosexual polygamy, while wrong and harmful in God's eyes, is tolerated to a limited degree by God in the Old Testament (e.g. Jacob with Leah and Rachel) because it deviates to a relatively small degree from His design.

At the other end of the scale, homosexuality and bestiality are the most harshly condemned sexual sins in the Bible because they deviate the furthest from the *"one flesh"* paradigm.

Knowing this helps us to understand why the God of Love speaks so forcefully against homosexual sin. His model is designed to bless us individually and corporately, but blessing cannot come from deviance.

With this in mind we will address the first of the four points of reference in Simon Peter's prophecy which identify the specific *"sensual"* and *"corrupt"* conduct of the last days heretics: The Days of Noah.

THE PETROS PROPHECY: SIMON PETER'S WARNING ABOUT THE HERESY OF THE LAST DAYS

Chapter Two:

THE DAYS OF NOAH

After the expulsion of Adam and Eve from the Garden of Eden, followed by a thousand years of increasing sin by their descendants, God poured out His wrath in the form of a global flood (described in Genesis 6-9), which the ancient Hebrew rabbis taught was triggered by homosexual and bestial "marriages" (Talmud, Genesis Rabbah 26:5:4). The Talmudic text reads "The generation of the Flood was not blotted out of the world until they had begun writing nuptial hymns for marriages between males or between man and beast."

The Talmud is an ancient book of rabbinical commentary on what we call the Old Testament, that at the time of its compilation was roughly equivalent to the notes and commentary in a Christian Study Bible. There is much controversy among Christians about using the Talmud as a source but we cite it here only to show how the ancient world's greatest authorities on their own native language interpreted the Hebrew Torah (the first five books of the Christian Bible).

A comparison of relevant passages of the Old and New Testaments in the Christian Bible to the above quote from the Talmud confirms its logic:

"Then the LORD saw that the wickedness of man was great on the earth, and that every intent of the thoughts of his heart was only evil continually. The LORD was sorry that He had made man on the earth, and He was grieved in His heart. The LORD said, 'I will blot out man whom I have created from the face of the land, from man to animals to creeping things and to birds of the sky; for I am sorry that I have made them.' But Noah found favor in the eyes of the LORD.....And God looked upon the earth, and, behold, it was corrupt; for all flesh had corrupted his way upon the earth" (Genesis 6:5-12).

"As it was in the days of Noah, so it will be at the coming of the Son of Man. For in the days before the flood, people were eating and drinking, marrying and giving in marriage, up to the day Noah entered the ark" (Matthew 24:37-38).

The ancient scholars of Hebrew who wrote the Talmud stated expressly what Jesus Himself alluded to. He warned that in the time leading to His return, wicked people would be "*marrying and giving in marriage*" "*as in the days of Noah*" (Matthew 24:38), when "*every intent of the thoughts of [their] heart was only evil continually*" (Genesis 6:5).

The truth of this would seem obvious if one simply asks the question, "What does marriage look like in a society of people whose every thought is evil continually?"

The main points here are that Biblical law and morality equate homosexuality with bestiality and that the human celebration of marriages based on these sexual perversions in the time of Noah represented the final insult to God triggering the Great Flood.

The common law crime of sodomy (rooted in Leviticus 18:22-23) is still on the books (though not enforced) in several U.S. States including Massachusetts, the first "gay marriage" state.[2] Specific sexual *acts* (eg oral or anal sex) are not emphasized as in modern statutory law, but instead two types of sexual *relationships* are prohibited: those between people of the same gender and those with animals, reflecting this same correlation in the Bible.

President Thomas Jefferson addressed this crime in his restatement of the common law and observed that of the two forms, homosexuality was the greater threat to society.[3]

GOD'S SYMBOL OF PROMISE BECOMES A HARBINGER OF WRATH BY FIRE

"And God said, This is the token of the covenant which I make between me and you and every living creature that is with you, for perpetual generations: I do set my bow in the cloud, and it shall be for a token of a covenant between me and the earth. And it shall come to pass, when I bring a cloud over the earth, that the bow shall be seen in the cloud: And I will remember my covenant, which is between me and you and every living creature of all flesh; and the waters shall no more become a flood to destroy all flesh. And the bow shall be in the cloud; and I will look upon it,

that I may remember the everlasting covenant between God and every living creature of all flesh that is upon the earth. And God said unto Noah, This is the token of the covenant, which I have established between me and all flesh that is upon the earth" (Genesis 9:18-17).

After the flood, God creates the *"bow"* (rainbow) as the symbol of His authority over the earth, specifically identified with His role as Judge of the Earth. With this symbol He promises never again to destroy the earth by flood (Genesis 9:15), knowing that He will bring a final destruction in the last days by fire:

*"[L]ong ago by God's word the heavens came into being and the earth was formed out of water and by water. By these waters also the world of that time was deluged and destroyed. **By the same word the present heavens and earth are reserved for fire**, being kept for the day of judgment and destruction of the ungodly"* (2 Peter 3:5-7).

The rainbow is intimately associated with the person and power of God. *"As the appearance of the rainbow in the clouds on a rainy day, so was the appearance of the surrounding radiance. Such was the appearance of the likeness of the glory of the LORD"* reads Ezekiel 1:28, and a rainbow emanates from His throne in heaven (Revelation 4:3).

It is not mere coincidence that the modern "gay" movement, so hostile to Biblical Christianity, has hijacked the symbol of the rainbow for itself. It is a hallmark of the

Antichrist spirit to claim God's throne for itself (2 Thessalonians 2:4).

THE CULTURE OF PERVERSION SURVIVES THE FLOOD

Just as modern Christian children from good homes can be morally corrupted by the worldly culture of their public schools, Noah's son Ham was apparently corrupted by the pre-flood homosexual culture of his time, and passed on his own moral weaknesses to his son Canaan. Canaan's defilement resulted in what seems best interpreted as the sexually molestation of his grandfather, Noah.

*"And Ham, the father of Canaan, saw the nakedness of his father, and told his two brethren without. And Shem and Japheth took a garment, and laid it upon both their shoulders, and went backward, and covered the nakedness of their father; and their faces were backward, and they saw not their father's nakedness. **And Noah awoke from his wine, and knew what his younger son had done unto him. And he said, Cursed be Canaan**"* (Genesis 9:22-25).

To *"uncover nakedness"* is a Biblical idiom for sexual intercourse. *"None of you shall approach any blood relative of his to uncover nakedness; I am the LORD"* states Leviticus 18:6. The Genesis passage has been interpreted by some to mean that Ham had sex with Noah's wife, producing Canaan by incest, a conclusion bolstered by Leviticus 20:11: *"The man that lies with his father's wife, has uncovered his father's nakedness."*

Alternately, the sin is interpreted to be the homosexual molestation of Noah by Canaan. We have chosen the latter interpretation, partly because this was the conclusion of Hebrew scholars of their own language,[4] but primarily because it more closely aligns with the pattern of conduct we have exposed in this study, and thus seems more plausible. Importantly, both alternatives fall within the list of "most-deviant" sexual sins expressly condemned by God in Leviticus 18.

Having been banished for his sin, Canaan and his descendants then brazenly colonize what we know today as the Holy Land and introduce ritual demon worship involving child sacrifice and sexual perversion (Leviticus 18, esp. 22-24). They also establish the cities of Sodom and Gomorrah (Genesis 10:19-20).

Again, the goal of the Antichrist spirit is to appropriate and defile what is most precious to God. We are of the view that the Holy Land of Israel is the same territory as the Land of Eden, and that Jerusalem is the site of the Garden of Eden. If so, this would explain why evil Canaan would take possession of this particular land of all the places on the earth he could have chosen.

Next we will address the second of four bases of reference provided by Simon Peter for identifying the sexual conduct associated with the heresy of the last days: Sodom and Gomorrah.

CHAPTER THREE:

SODOM AND GOMORRAH

The second inclusion-by-reference in Simon Peter's prophecy about the last days heresy is to the story of Sodom and Gomorrah. By the time Sodom and Gomorrah emerged in the Biblical chronology, sexual perversion had dramatically increased in the post-flood world, and so God provided a warning to humanity in the form of a foretaste of the wrath to come. That warning dramatically showcases the homosexual sin of Sodom.

In Genesis 19, God destroys Sodom and Gomorrah with fire and brimstone, foreshadowing the last-days destruction of the earth (2 Peter 2:6, Jude 1:7). The final insult to God is the attempted homosexual rape of His two angelic witnesses whom He sent to Sodom to confirm its wickedness (Gen 19:4-5).

"And there came two angels to Sodom at even; and Lot sat in the gate of Sodom: and Lot seeing them rose up to meet them; and he bowed himself with his face toward the ground; And he said, Behold now, my lords, turn in, I pray you, into your servant's house, and tarry all night, and wash your feet, and ye shall rise up early, and go on your ways. And they said, Nay; but we will abide in the street all night. And he pressed upon them greatly; and they turned in unto him, and entered into his house; and he made

them a feast, and did bake unleavened bread, and they did eat. But before they lay down, the men of the city, even the men of Sodom, compassed the house round, both old and young, all the people from every quarter: And they called unto Lot, and said unto him, Where are the men which came in to thee this night? bring them out unto us, that we may know them.

"And Lot went out at the door unto them, and shut the door after him, And said, I pray you, brethren, do not so wickedly. 8Behold now, I have two daughters which have not known man; let me, I pray you, bring them out unto you, and do ye to them as is good in your eyes: only unto these men do nothing; for therefore came they under the shadow of my roof. And they said, Stand back. And they said again, This one fellow came in to sojourn, and he will needs be a judge: now will we deal worse with thee, than with them. And they pressed sore upon the man, even Lot, and came near to break the door. But the men put forth their hand, and pulled Lot into the house to them, and shut to the door. And they smote the men that were at the door of the house with blindness, both small and great: so that they wearied themselves to find the door" (Genesis 19:1-10).

" Then the LORD rained upon Sodom and upon Gomorrah brimstone and fire from the LORD out of heaven; And he overthrew those cities, and all the plain, and all the inhabitants of the cities, and that which grew upon the ground...And it came to pass, when God destroyed the cities of the plain, that God remembered Abraham, and sent Lot out of the midst of the overthrow, when he

overthrew the cities in the which Lot dwelt" (Genesis 19:24-29).

Importantly, the incineration of Sodom and Gomorrah is completely unique in Biblical history. God's intentional association of homosexuality with the outpouring of His wrath by fire is absolutely unmistakable, as is His warning that it was simply a preview of the last days.

"He condemned the cities of Sodom and Gomorrah to destruction by reducing them to ashes, having made them an example to those who would live ungodly lives thereafter" (2 Peter 2:6).

"Sodom and Gomorrah and the cities around them, since they in the same way as these indulged in gross immorality and went after strange flesh, are exhibited as an example in undergoing the punishment of eternal fire" (Jude 1:7).

THE SECOND WITNESS OF SODOM'S SIN

In Judges 19, ala Sodom, the attempted homosexual rape of a Levite by the Benjamites of Gibeah leads to civil war among the Hebrew tribes.

Frequently, God gives special emphasis to His teachings by sending two witnesses. A we noted above, this occurred when God sent two angels to bear witness to Sodom's homosexual sin before the outpouring of His wrath. But there are also two separate *incidents* in the Bible which bear witness to the special correlation of homosexuality with apostasy and judgment. The first is, of course, Genesis 19. The second witness is Judges 19. The full text of both passages is included in Appendix A, but we have excerpted a portion of Judges 19 here to show the similarity to Genesis 19:

Judges 19:22-24: *"Now as they were making their hearts merry, behold, the men of the city, certain sons of Belial, beset the house round about, and beat at the door, and spake to the master of the house, the old man, saying, Bring forth the man that came into thine house, that we may know him. And the man, the master of the house, went out unto them, and said unto them, Nay, my brethren, nay, I pray you, do not so wickedly; seeing that this man is come into mine house, do not this folly. Behold, here is my daughter a maiden, and his concubine; them I will bring out now, and humble ye them, and do with them what seems good unto you: but unto this man do not so vile a thing."*

Readers of both passages will be struck by the clear parallel in the two stories, the primary common elements being the mobs of predatory homosexual men insistent on raping the male guest(s), the offering of female substitutes as the lesser evil, and the severe consequence to society from the behavior of the homosexuals.

The differences in the stories highlight the importance of the common elements but also add meaning to the lesson. For example, the fact that the object of the homosexual's lust in Judges 19 is a Levite is significant as the Levites were the tribe of priests who served as Old Testament intermediaries between God and man, and thus the offense was against both God and man simultaneously -- a violation of the first and the second great commandment.

THE REPROBATE MIND

The condemnation of homosexual perversion in the Old Testament continues in the New Testament under Christ. For example, in 1 Timothy 1, homosexuals are equated with murderers, slavers and perjurers (v.9-10).

More damningly, Romans 1 singles out homosexuality to exemplify the "reprobate mind," and identify the period of apostasy preceding the return of Christ. In it the Apostle Paul expounds on the theme of natural law from the Biblical perspective, but also frames the discussion in an end-times context:

"For the wrath of God is revealed from heaven against all ungodliness and unrighteousness of men who suppress the truth in unrighteousness, because that which is known about God is evident within them; for God made it evident to them. For since the creation of the world His invisible attributes, His eternal power and divine nature, have been clearly seen, being understood through what has been made, so that they are without excuse ...Therefore God gave them over in the lusts of their hearts to impurity, so that their bodies would be dishonored among them. For they exchanged the truth of God for a lie, and worshipped and served the creature rather than the Creator, who is blessed forever. Amen. For this reason

God gave them over to degrading passions; for their women exchanged the natural function for that which is unnatural, and in the same way also the men abandoned the natural function of the woman and burned in their desire toward one another, men with men committing indecent acts and receiving in their own persons the due penalty of their error" (Romans 1:18-27).

The phrase "*wrath of God…revealed from heaven"* invokes both the incineration of Sodom and the coming destruction in the last days and associates it unmistakably with homosexuality.

Moreover, the characteristics of the end-times apostate culture are portrayed as a direct consequence of the embrace of homosexual perversion by the society (note especially the last sentence of the following passage).

"*And just as they did not see fit to acknowledge God any longer, God gave them over to a depraved mind, to do those things which are not proper, being filled with all unrighteousness, wickedness, greed, evil; full of envy, murder, strife, deceit, malice; they are gossips, slanderers, haters of God, insolent, arrogant, boastful, inventors of evil, disobedient to parents, without understanding, untrustworthy, unloving, unmerciful. And although they know the ordinance of God, that those who practice such things are worthy of death, they not only do the same, <u>but also give hearty approval to those who practice them</u>"* (Romans 1:28-32).

Again, keeping in mind that God frequently provides two witnesses to emphasize an important teaching, compare the list of apostate conduct in Romans 1 with the only other place in scripture one is found: 2 Timothy 3:1-5:

"But realize this, that in the last days difficult times will come. For men will be lovers of self, lovers of money, boastful, arrogant, revilers, disobedient to parents, ungrateful, unholy, unloving, irreconcilable, malicious gossips, without self-control, brutal, haters of good, treacherous, reckless, conceited, lovers of pleasure rather than lovers of God, holding to a form of godliness, although they have denied its power; Avoid such men as these."

Lastly, note the last days context of the 2 Timothy passage. Take together these two Biblical witnesses clearly warn that the societal embrace of homosexuality will define the culture of the end, and the final warning in both passages is for believers to shun that culture.

SODOM AND THE KINGDOM OF THE ANTICHRIST

Scripture warns that the last days Kingdom of the Antichrist will be defined by homosexuality and polytheism, also known as religious pluralism.

Revelation 6 warns that the end-times Antichrist (a counterfeit version of the true Messiah as seen in Revelation 19:11-16) will ride forth on a white horse *"conquering and to conquer"* holding aloft a *"bow"* (likely

God's symbol of authority, the rainbow) (v.2).

"Then I saw when the Lamb broke one of the seven seals, and I heard one of the four living creatures saying as with a voice of thunder, 'Come.' I looked, and behold, a white horse, and he who sat on it had a bow; and a crown was given to him, and he went out conquering and to conquer. When He broke the second seal, I heard the second living creature saying, 'Come.' And another, a red horse, went out; and to him who sat on it, it was granted to take peace from the earth, and that men would slay one another; and a great sword was given to him. When He broke the third seal, I heard the third living creature saying, 'Come' I looked, and behold, a black horse; and he who sat on it had a pair of scales in his hand....When the Lamb broke the fourth seal, I heard the voice of the fourth living creature saying, 'Come.' I looked, and behold, an ashen horse; and he who sat on it had the name Death; and Hades was following with him'" (Revelation 6:1-8).

Chapter 6 of Revelation closely parallels a portion of the Olivet Discourse in Matt 24, Luke 21, and Mark 13, in which Jesus summarized the sequences of end-times events before His return. The Four Horsemen of the Apocalypse represent the four phases or aspects of what Jesus calls "*the beginning of sorrows*" (labor pains) just before the start of the tribulation (Matthew 24:4-8).

The white horse represents the Antichrist, and the "*bow*" which he holds is almost certainly the rainbow. Remember that the Antichrist is an imposter who seeks to deceive the world into thinking he is the messiah. The real Christ will return "*in the clouds*" at His second coming (Matthew 24:30), and on a white horse. Revelation 19:11 states "*And I saw heaven opened, and behold, a white horse, and He who sat on it is called Faithful and True, and in righteousness He judges and wages war.*"

Remember also that the rainbow, which God set "*in the clouds*" after the great flood (Genesis 9:13) is the symbol of God's authority over the earth and evidence of His presence (Ezekiel 1:28 and Revelation 4:3). The Antichrist will apparently appropriate the symbol of the rainbow for himself as part of his claim to deity.

The crown represents the authority which God allows the Antichrist to briefly wield.

Interestingly, while the crown is "*given to him*" the rainbow was not, but was something he already "*had*," or claimed possession of, suggesting (especially in the context of this study) an association with the global LGBT movement. Further to that point, the Antichrist goes forth "*conquering and to conquer*" which is traditionally interpreted to mean military conquest but is more precisely described in Revelation 13:7: "*It was also given to him to make war with the saints and to overcome them, and authority over every tribe and people and tongue and nation was given to him.*"

The LGBT movement is unarguably warring against Christianity across the world today and winning nearly every battle. The few nations which continue to offer strong resistance, such as Uganda and Russia find themselves "coincidentally" the subjects of intense hostility from the "international community," albeit not always overtly related to the homosexual issue.

Importantly, when the Antichrist takes power he will deceive the world with lies that are already largely embraced by non-believers: *"The coming of the lawless one will be in accordance with how Satan works. He will use all sorts of displays of power through signs and wonders that serve the lie, <u>and all the ways that wickedness deceives those who are perishing</u>. They perish because they refused to love the truth and so be saved"* (2 Thessalonians 2:9-10).

One of those lies is the normalcy of sexual perversion, but another is "religious pluralism," the idea that all religions are equal and equally subservient to secular humanist government.[5]

Revelation 11:7-8 identifies Jerusalem under the reign of the Antichrist as *"spiritually...called Sodom and Egypt"* meaning that it is known for homosexuality and polytheism:

*"I will grant authority to my two witnesses, and they will prophesy for twelve hundred and sixty days, clothed in sackcloth....When they have finished their testimony, the beast that comes up out of the abyss will make war with them, and overcome them and kill them. **And their dead bodies will lie in the street of the great city which spiritually is called Sodom and Egypt, where also their Lord was crucified.**"*

Lastly, to remove any doubt as to the relationship of last-days homosexual sin to the Antichrist Kingdom, the metaphor used by the Bible to encapsulate the full meaning of the Great Day of God's Wrath is the "*harvest*" of the grapes of Sodom:

"*And another angel came out of the temple, crying with a loud voice to him that sat on the cloud, Thrust in thy sickle, and reap: for the time is come for thee to reap; for the harvest of the earth is ripe...Thrust in thy sharp sickle, and gather the clusters of the vine of the earth; for her grapes are fully ripe. And the angel thrust in his sickle into the earth, and gathered the vine of the earth, and cast it into the great winepress of the wrath of God*" (Revelation 14:15-20).

"[*Their grapes come] from the vine of Sodom and from the fields of Gomorrah. Their grapes are filled with poison, and their clusters with bitterness. Their wine is the venom of serpents, the deadly poison of cobras*" (Deuteronomy 32:32-33).

THE PETROS PROPHECY: SIMON PETER'S WARNING ABOUT THE HERESY OF THE LAST DAYS

CHAPTER FOUR:

LOT'S LIFE CIRCUMSTANCES

"He rescued righteous Lot, oppressed by the sensual conduct of unprincipled men (for by what he saw and heard that righteous man, while living among them, felt his righteous soul tormented day after day by their lawless deeds)" (2 Peter 2:7-8).

THE PERSONAL COSTS

The third of four reference points of Simon Peter's prophecy that define the specific nature of the "*sensual conduct*" and "*lawless deeds*" of the last days heretics relates to Abraham's nephew Lot. Lot was a long-time resident of the City of Sodom but did not embrace its culture.

Peter declares him "*righteous*" which seems strange given that Lot offered his two virgin daughters to the homosexual mob demanding to have sex with his male guests in Genesis 19, but that serves to underscore the greater weight of shame attributable to homosexuality in the Bible.

For the purposes of our study it is enough that the conduct that aggravated Lot -- the conduct attributable to the last days heretics in Simon Peter's prophecy, is unmistakably homosexual sin.

Lot's righteousness was defined not by his deeds but the state of his heart. And thus we are reminded that repentance and an unshakable spiritual allegiance to God can preserve our eternal salvation from even the most egregious of sins, though we cannot escape the natural consequences of our deeds in the physical realm. This cause and effect (sowing and reaping) phenomenon is true for everyone individually and for society as a whole.

One consequence of Lot's sins, for example, was that the two nations founded through incest with his daughters, the Ammonites and Moabites respectively, were forever branded as *Mamzers*, and restricted from inclusion in the assembly of the Hebrews (Deuteronomy 23).

SEXUAL SIN CAN CORRUPT EVEN THE WISEST OF MEN

In 1 Kings 11, Solomon's reintroduction of Canaanite ritual child sacrifice and sexual perversion, including homosexuality, caused God to take the Kingdom of Israel away from him and divide it in two (v. 5-13).

Many Christians are unaware that in his later years, "wise" King Solomon succumbed to sexual perversion and sinned greatly against the Lord.

"For when Solomon was old, his wives turned his heart away after other gods; and his heart was not wholly devoted to the LORD his God, as the heart of David his father had been. **For Solomon went after Ashtoreth the goddess of the Sidonians and after Milcom the detestable idol of the Ammonites.** *Solomon did what was evil in the sight of the LORD, and did not follow the LORD fully, as David his father had done.* **Then Solomon built a high place for Chemosh the detestable idol of Moab, on the mountain which is east of Jerusalem, and for Molech the detestable idol of the sons of Ammon.** *Thus also he did for all his foreign wives, who burned incense and sacrificed to their gods"* (1 Kings 11:5-8).

In other words, King Solomon allowed and might even have participated in rampant sexual perversion and the murder of innocent children in sacrifice to demons on the Mount of Olives. While Solomon apparently repented later in his life, as his authorship of the Book of Ecclesiastes suggests, he nevertheless suffered severely for his sins.

"Now the LORD was angry with Solomon because his heart was turned away from the LORD, the God of Israel, who had appeared to him twice, and had commanded him concerning this thing, that he should not go after other gods; but he did not observe what the LORD had commanded. So the LORD said to Solomon, **'Because you have done this, and you have not kept My covenant and My statutes, which I have commanded you, I will surely tear the kingdom from you, and will give it to your servant.** *'Nevertheless I will not do it in your days for the sake of your father David, but I will tear it out of the hand*

of your son. 'However, I will not tear away all the kingdom, but I will give one tribe to your son for the sake of My servant David and for the sake of Jerusalem which I have chosen'" (1 Kings 11:9-13).

Thus, due primarily to sexual sin, the Kingdom of David was divided in two: the House of Judah (Judah and Benjamin) and the House of Israel (the other Ten Tribes).[6]

JOSIAH'S RIGHTEOUS EXAMPLE

In 2 Kings 23, Josiah is named as the most righteous of all the Kings (v 25) in part because he "*broke down the houses of the Sodomites who were in the House of the Lord*" (v.7) -- ending what Solomon had begun 300 years before.

Central to the worship of the demon gods of the heathens were fertility rituals including practices involving sexual perversion, which is why God always equates idolatry with adultery in the Bible. As you read the following description of Josiah's reforms, remember that much of this idolatry was occurring in or near the Temple of God:

"Then the king [Josiah] commanded Hilkiah the high priest and the priests of the second order and the doorkeepers, to bring out of the temple of the LORD all the vessels that were made for Baal, for Asherah, and for all the host of heaven; and he burned them outside Jerusalem in the fields of the Kidron, and carried their ashes to Bethel. He did away with the idolatrous priests whom the kings of

Judah had appointed to burn incense in the high places in the cities of Judah and in the surrounding area of Jerusalem, also those who burned incense to Baal, to the sun and to the moon and to the constellations and to all the host of heaven. He brought out the Asherah from the house of the LORD outside Jerusalem to the brook Kidron, and burned it at the brook Kidron, and ground it to dust, and threw its dust on the graves of the common people.

"He also broke down the houses of the male cult prostitutes which were in the house of the LORD, where the women were weaving hangings for the Asherah. Then he brought all the priests from the cities of Judah, and defiled the high places where the priests had burned incense, from Geba to Beersheba; and he broke down the high places of the gates which were at the entrance of the gate of Joshua the governor of the city, which were on one's left at the city gate. Nevertheless the priests of the high places did not go up to the altar of the LORD in Jerusalem, but they ate unleavened bread among their brothers.

"He also defiled Topheth, which is in the valley of the son of Hinnom, that no man might make his son or his daughter pass through the fire for Molech. He did away with the horses which the kings of Judah had given to the sun, at the entrance of the house of the LORD, by the chamber of Nathan-melech the official, which was in the precincts; and he burned the chariots of the sun with fire. The altars which were on the roof, the upper chamber of Ahaz, which the kings of Judah had made, and the altars which Manasseh had made in the two courts of the house

of the LORD, the king broke down; and he smashed them there and threw their dust into the brook Kidron.

"The high places which were before Jerusalem, which were on the right of the mount of destruction which Solomon the king of Israel had built for Ashtoreth the abomination of the Sidonians, and for Chemosh the abomination of Moab, and for Milcom the abomination of the sons of Ammon, the king defiled. He broke in pieces the sacred pillars and cut down the Asherim and filled their places with human bones."

The *"sacred pillars"* and *"Asherim"* mentioned in this passage were fertility symbols, most likely including giant phalluses carved from oak trees (e.g. Ezekiel 16:17), which were a feature of the *"sacred oak groves"* often found on the *"high places"* where the demons were worshipped through male and female prostitution. The ritual of "kissing under the mistletoe" derives from this ancient pagan association of sex with oak trees, as mistletoe is a parasite most commonly found in oak groves.

There is nothing new under the sun, and today, just as in the Old Testament, sexual sin defiles God's people and the land on which they live. However, the Good News is that everyone, including homosexuals can be healed and delivered by Christ.

HEALING AND DELIVERANCE

1 Corinthians, Chapter 6 warns that neither homosexuals (nor transsexuals) can inherit the Kingdom of Heaven, but they can be saved and healed of homosexuality by Christ:

*"[D]o you not know that the unrighteous will not inherit the kingdom of God? Do not be deceived; **neither** fornicators, nor idolaters, nor adulterers, nor **effeminate, nor homosexuals**, nor thieves, nor the covetous, nor drunkards, nor revilers, nor swindlers, **will inherit the kingdom of God**. <u>Such were some of you</u>; but you were washed, but you were sanctified, but you were justified in the name of the Lord Jesus Christ and in the Spirit of our God"* (1 Corinthians 6:9-11).

The simple, powerful truth of God is that He can heal homosexuals and deliver them from their bondage to sexual sin. It is a fact of Biblical history! In declaring that promise, this passage also reveals that former homosexuals were some of the earliest members of the church.

Thus, those who accept the lie of the modern age that homosexuals cannot change insult God and deny the truth of His Word. To these people, which sadly includes an increasing number of Christians, James' warning is especially relevant:

"You adulterous people, don't you know that friendship with the world means enmity against God? Therefore, anyone who chooses to be a friend of the world becomes an enemy of God" (James 4:4).

Consider further the implications of the lie that homosexuality is innate and unchangeable, especially for children who struggle with same-sex attraction due to sexual molestation or gender identity disorder -- frequently from Christian homes. Consider the burden of shame and fear carried by young people who struggle with same-sex attraction disorder (SSAD) and the effect on them of being told by the "experts" that they have NO HOPE of ever being healed of it. Is it any wonder that so many "gay" kids commit suicide?

Further, what is the implication for those who help perpetuate that disheartening lie?

"[W]hoever causes one of these little ones who believe in Me to stumble, it would be better for him to have a heavy millstone hung around his neck, and to be drowned in the depth of the sea" (Matthew 18:6).

Every believer in this age should always be ready to rebut that lie and offer real hope to those who struggle with homosexual sin by citing 1 Corinthians 6:9-11.

CHAPTER FIVE:

THE WAY OF BALAAM

The fourth and final of Peter's historical references that define the nature of the last days heresy is "the way of Balaam," emphasizing the destructiveness to society of sexual sin.

THE SOCIAL CONSEQUENCES

[T]hey have gone astray, having followed <u>the way of Balaam</u>....speaking out arrogant words of vanity they entice by fleshly desires, by sensuality, those who barely escape from the ones who live in error, promising them freedom while they themselves are slaves of corruption; for by what a man is overcome, by this he is enslaved" (2 Peter 2:1-19).

Balaam was the magician who (in Numbers 22-24) refused Moabite King Balak's command to curse the Hebrews out of fear of God. But, as stated in Revelation 2:14-15, Balaam advised Balak that the same result could be accomplished by involving the Hebrews in sexual sin. *"Balaam...taught Balak to cast a stumblingblock before the children of Israel, to eat things sacrificed unto idols, and to commit fornication."*

Thus, *"the people began to play the harlot with the daughters of Moab. For they invited the people to the sacrifices of their gods, and the people ate and bowed down to their gods"* (Numbers 25:1-2).

As we have noted, the Canaanite religion which Moab had adopted involved extreme sexual perversion, including homosexuality.

The Defilement of the Land

In Leviticus 18, God identifies incest, homosexuality and bestiality as the sins which cause the land to *"vomit out its inhabitants"* (v25). Even in this dark context homosexuality is singled out for special condemnation as *"an abomination"* (v.22).

In what is probably the most challenging Biblical passage of all, Deuteronomy 20:16-18, God tells the Hebrew people to completely eliminate the Canaanite inhabitants of the Holy Land. His explanation why is detailed in Leviticus 18:24-30.

"Do not defile yourselves by any of these things; for by all these the nations which I am casting out before you have become defiled. 'For the land has become defiled, therefore I have brought its punishment upon it, so the land has spewed out its inhabitants. But as for you, you are to keep My statutes and My judgments and shall not do any of these abominations, neither the native, nor the alien who sojourns among you (for the men of the land

who have been before you have done all these abominations, and the land has become defiled); so that the land will not spew you out, should you defile it, as it has spewed out the nation which has been before you. 'For whoever does any of these abominations, those persons who do so shall be cut off from among their people. 'Thus you are to keep My charge, that you do not practice any of the abominable customs which have been practiced before you, so as not to defile yourselves with them; I am the LORD your God."

It is certainly not within our right to judge God. We can only rest in the assurance that, by definition, whatever God does is justified. Importantly, however, his use of genocide to punish sexual perversion is instructive as to His perspective of the relative gravity of human sins, as is His admonition not to tolerate these forms of sexual conduct by any persons in the society, even "*the sojourner among you.*"

Of course, neither does this justify hatred or violence against homosexuals. To quote from one of my articles:

> "Under the New Covenant by which Christ has instituted an era of grace for those who belong to Him (John 1:17; Romans 11:25) believers are freed from the law of sin and death (Romans 8:2), instructed to love the lost, even our enemies (Matthew 5:44) and leave vengeance to Him (Romans 12:19). Our weapons are not physical, but spiritual (2 Corinthians 10:3-5)…under the new

covenant it is Christ Himself who *"judges and makes war"* against the wicked (Revelation 19:11-16)....

"Our instruction from Christ is to lead sinners to Him (Matthew 28:19-20) so that they may be spared the terrible consequence of their sin — both in this life and in eternity — through the acceptance of His sacrifice on the cross (Romans 10:9-10). If they reject Christ their blood is upon their own heads but we have done our job (Ezekiel 3:18-19)."

HOMOSEXUALITY AS A TOOL OF THE ANTICHRIST

In Daniel 11, Antiochus IV Epiphanes, the clearest Antichrist prototype of the Bible, uses homosexuality to corrupt Hebrew male youth in his plan to turn the Jews away from God (v.21-39, see also 1 Maccabees 1, esp v.14-16).

"Forces from him will arise, desecrate the sanctuary fortress, and do away with the regular sacrifice. And they will set up the abomination of desolation. **By smooth words he will turn to godlessness those who act wickedly toward the covenant, but the people who know their God will display strength and take action.** *Those who have insight among the people will give understanding to the many ...Some of those who have insight will fall, in order to refine, purge and make them pure until the end-times;*

because it is still to come at the appointed time. Then the king will do as he pleases, and he will exalt and magnify himself above every god and will speak monstrous things against the God of gods; and he will prosper until the indignation is finished, for that which is decreed will be done. He will show no regard for the gods of his fathers or for the desire of women, nor will he show regard for any other god; for he will magnify himself above them all" (Daniel 11:31-37).

Daniel does not specify the process by which those who disregard the covenant are turned to godlessness, but the apocryphal book of 1 Maccabees 1 does. The Books of the Maccabees are not inspired scripture, but they are highly reliable historical records, and provide key details of the events described in summary by Daniel. The reader is encouraged to read the entirely of 1 Maccabees 1 for context.

> "Antiochus Epiphanes began to rule….At that time, some renegade Israelites emerged. These people went against their ancestral laws and encouraged many other Jews to join them. They spoke up, saying, 'Let's make an agreement with the Gentiles around us'…. **Consequently, they built a gymnasium in Jerusalem, following Gentile custom.**…They **joined with Gentiles and gave themselves over to an evil course**…Then King Antiochus sent word throughout his entire kingdom that everyone should act like one people, giving up their local customs….**They were supposed to**

> make themselves repulsive to God by doing unclean and improper acts. All of this was intended to make them forget the Law and change its regulations....
>
> "The king's inspectors drove Israel into hiding in every place of refuge they had available....they set up a disgusting and destructive thing on the altar for entirely burned offerings in the sanctuary....When they found the Law scrolls, they tore them to pieces and burned them. If anyone was caught in possession of a copy of the covenant scroll or if anyone kept to the Law, that person was condemned to death by royal decree.... In keeping with the decree, they killed women who had circumcised their sons. They hanged the infant boys from their mothers' necks" (1 Maccabees 1:10-61).

The Greek "gymnasium," where young men engaged in sporting events in the nude, was a center of homosexuality and one of the reasons sodomy became known throughout the entire western world as "Greek love." In his article, *Homosexuality & the Maccabean Revolt*, Catholic scholar Patrick G.D. Riley notes:

> The all-male athletic club known as the gymnasium was notorious in the ancient world as a nestingplace for pederasty. Socrates himself was susceptible to it, as we learn in the *Charmides*. The lovers of boys came to the

gymnasium in crowds, as Plato notes in that dialogue and in the *Euthydemus*. Plutarch mentions it in the *Erotikos*. Hence the gymnasium, with its sexual seductions, was bound to arouse alarm when it arrived in Jerusalem and "attracted the noblest young men" of Israel (2 Macc. 4:12). What follows that phrase bears this out. The original Greek of the text of 2 Maccabees continues with a pun: *hypotasson hypo petason*, which literally means "subduing [these noble young Jews] under the petason," the broad-brimmed hat of Hermes worn by naked Greek athletes. But in the Church's traditional Latin translation, known as the Vulgate, St. Jerome renders this *in lupanaribus ponere*, that is, "to put in brothels"

...[They] joined themselves to the Gentiles. In the Greek, this has a strong connotation of sexual union. The verb, *zeugizein*, means "to yoke in pairs," a graphic metaphor for sexual union. It is used in a love-passage from second-century B.C. Alexandria, hence contemporary with the Maccabees, in a context implying copulation. Since the Greek gymnasium was traditionally exclusive to males, and since the histories present the Jerusalem gymnasium as male-only, the sexual union can only be homosexual. (*New Oxford Review*, September 1997).

Thus, with these examples we can recognize the clear Scriptural warning not only to individuals but to societies as well.

CONCLUSION:

WILL THE CHURCH HEED THE WARNING?

Simon Peter's prophecy is one component of a larger story, but it is an important one.

In this short book we took a deeper look into 2 Peter 2 than the modern church may be comfortable with, but in searching out the significance of his four reference points: Noah's flood, Sodom's incineration, Lot's vexation of spirit, and Balaam's error, we now know that the "*destructive heresies*" of the last days, defined by "*sensuality*" and "*the lust of defiling passions*" (v.1-19), is an unmistakable warning about "gay theology" and the legitimization of sexual promiscuity, especially homosexuality, in the church and the larger society.

As we conclude this study let us pause to recognize what is meant by "*despising authority*" in 2 Peter 2:10, regarding "*those who indulge the flesh in its corrupt desires and despise authority.*"

What authority?

It is the authority of God's Word and those who espouse it.

"*Those who indulge the flesh...*" clearly describes the proponents of "gay theology," especially, it would seem, the political activists of the "lesbian, gay, bisexual, transgender" (LGBT) lobby Their community is largely defined by "*indulgence of the flesh in corrupt desires.*" This is both a spiritual and a political observation: one that triggers both the Christian duty to be good stewards of the society we live in, and our duty to defend the Truth of Christ.

"*Many will follow their sensuality, and because of them the way of the truth will be maligned*" reads 2 Peter 2:2. Could any phrase more perfectly capture the essence of the "culture war" in our age in which LGBT activists and self-declared "gay Christians" and their surrogates, champion the sexual revolution while declaring Biblical Christianity to be a religion of hate? It is an overt goal of their political tactics to ensure that the way of truth is maligned, and its authority is despised!

And doesn't this entire second chapter of 2 Peter describe America and the West today? -- a hyper-sexualized culture of people "*reveling*" in self-deception, rationalizing that they are "*born as creatures of instinct,*" driven by insatiable lust and full of boastful "pride" about it, enticing others to join them in what they call "sexual freedom" but which is actually bondage and addiction?

We find in "gay theology" the subtlety and craftiness that the apostle warns against, and in the "gay" movement an army of proponents who "*entice by fleshly desires, by sensuality...promising freedom while they themselves are slaves of corruption*," perfectly exemplifying 2 Peter 2:18-19.

In tandem with "gay theology," and a leading contributor to recidivism among ex-"gays," is antinomianism, the false doctrine of grace-as-license-to-sin – falsely "*promising freedom*"-- that Paul systematically debunks in Romans 2-8. (This topic is somewhat beyond the scope of this book, but is addressed in article six in Appendix B, under the title " 'Gay' Recovery, Recidivism and Grace.")

Again, we have demonstrated that Simon Peter provided a very stark and clear warning about the last days heresy of "gay theology." And we have shown that the compilation of all key scriptures on homosexuality (including Simon Peter's prophecy), when taken as a whole, constitute a message greater than the sum of its parts – far bigger than any political implications: a warning that the rise of homosexuality as a widespread cultural phenomenon will be a hallmark of the Antichrist Kingdom and herald the imminent unleashing of the wrath of God.

We must therefore consider with all gravity the practical ramifications of these facts. "Gay theology" is infiltrating the Christian church at an alarming pace. Many believers, fearful of being called "haters," are trivializing the threat by calling homosexuality "just another sin." But from Genesis to Revelation, the Bible teaches that homosexuality is NOT "just another sin." It is a symbol of extreme rebellion against God and harbinger of His wrath.

It is our belief that the emergence of widespread homosexuality and its celebration by the world is designed to test the faithfulness of the church to God's Word. It is, in a sense, a "dress rehearsal" for the Mark of the Beast, as indeed "sexual orientation" laws in parts of our economy today prohibit "buying or selling" without first accepting the normalcy of homosexuality as a precondition -- eerily foreshadowing the consequence of resisting the Antichrist in Revelation 13:17.

Courage in defending the Bible regarding homosexuality is certainly not a "salvation issue," which fact helps the timid rationalize their avoidance of the topic. Yet this is precisely why it serves God's purpose as a litmus-test.

"He who is faithful in a very little thing is faithful also in much; and he who is unrighteous in a very little thing is unrighteous also in much" (Luke 16:10).

If a Christian is unable to remain faithful to Biblical truth when all he will suffer is the disapproval of the world or the loss of a job, how can he be expected to stand with Christ when the cost is his life? (Revelation 12:11). As Jeremiah 12:5 puts it:

"If you have run with footmen and they have tired you out, Then how can you compete with horses? If you fall down in a land of peace, How will you do in the thicket of the Jordan?"

As we ponder God's unmistakable warning about homosexuality in the light of current events and present day church compromises, the words of Jesus ring with special significance: *"When the Son of Man comes, will He find faith on the earth?"* (Luke 18:8).

It is incumbent upon believers who have learned the truth on these matters to warn the church against the heresy of "gay theology" and to boldly and forcefully advocate for the

Biblical worldview on sexuality and the *"one-flesh"* paradigm.

While there are many pro-family resources available on the Internet to refute this dangerous modern heresy, every believer should at minimum be familiar with the following essential points.

- Not a single passage in the entire Bible portrays homosexuality positively (though "Gay" heretics twist a few verses to create a false impression – for example, David was an enthusiastic heterosexual, notwithstanding his brotherly love for Jonathan -- 1 Samuel 18:1, 2 Samuel 11).

- Jesus unequivocally condemned ALL sexual sin including homosexuality by affirming the *"one flesh"* paradigm of Genesis (Matthew 19:4-6).

- Condemnation of homosexuality predates the Mosaic code and is reaffirmed in the New Testament, so it bears no relation to the ban on eating oysters, mixing fabrics, or other supposedly "repealed" laws of the Bible.

- "Eunuch" is not a synonym for "homosexual" in the Bible but means any man who has been castrated or who practices strict celibacy (Deuteronomy 23:1, Matthew 19:12).

Further study is warranted but we will leave that to the conscience of the reader to take upon him or herself.

Peter ends his second letter with the following admonition and final caution about the last days heresy. This will be our final word on the matter, and we join him in invoking this blessing upon you.

*"[B]e diligent to be found by Him in peace, spotless and blameless, and regard the patience of our Lord as salvation; just as also our beloved brother Paul, according to the wisdom given him, wrote to you, as also in all his letters, speaking in them of these things, in which are some things hard to understand, **which the untaught and unstable distort, as they do also the rest of the Scriptures, to their own destruction.** You therefore, beloved, knowing this beforehand, be on your guard so that you are not carried away by the error of unprincipled men and fall from your own steadfastness, but grow in the grace and knowledge of our Lord and Savior Jesus Christ"* (2 Peter 3:14-18).

Appendix A:

The Full Text of Biblical Passages Cited in this Book.

It is hoped that anyone interested in the claims of this book would have their own Bible, but for those who don't, we are including the full text of the relevant passages here to provide context for the scriptures we have cited. "Full text" can itself be a term of art, since it involves a somewhat subjective determination of what is relevant, but we've done our best to include enough context to help the average reader recognize the validity of our assertions.

All the passages directly related to the Biblical case against homosexuality are presented in the order in which they appear in the Bible. Passages which explain or expand upon a particular theological truth (such as Jesus' New Testament reaffirmation of the "One Flesh Paradigm" of Genesis 2:24), and texts central to the flow of our argument (such as the Romans 1:18) are presented where they best illuminate the Biblical message on the point in question. The specific text we have cited is underlined.

TRUTH VS ERROR: ROMANS 1:18.

16For I am not ashamed of the gospel of Christ: for it is the power of God unto salvation to every one that believeth; to the Jew first, and also to the Greek. 17For therein is the righteousness of God revealed from faith to faith: as it is written, The just shall live by faith. 18For the wrath of God is revealed from heaven against all ungodliness and unrighteousness of <u>men, who hold the truth in unrighteousness [our translation: "They suppress the truth in unrighteousness"]</u>; 19Because that which may be known of God is manifest in them; for God hath shewed it unto them. 20For the invisible things of him from the creation of the world are clearly seen, being understood by the things that are made, even his eternal power and Godhead; so that they are without excuse: 21Because that, when they knew God, they glorified him not as God, neither were thankful; but became vain in their imaginations, and their foolish heart was darkened. 22Professing themselves to be wise, they became fools, 23And changed the glory of the uncorruptible God into an image made like to corruptible man, and to birds, and fourfooted beasts, and creeping things.

THE BIRTH OF HERESY: GENESIS 3:1-7.

1<u>Now the serpent was more subtil than any beast of the field which the LORD God had made. And he said unto the woman, Yea, hath God said, Ye shall not eat of every tree of the garden?</u> 2And the woman said unto the serpent, We may eat of the fruit of the trees of the garden: 3But of the fruit of the tree which is in the midst of the garden, God hath said, Ye shall not eat of it, neither shall ye touch it, lest ye die. 4And the serpent said unto the woman, Ye shall not surely die: 5For God doth know that in the day ye eat thereof, then your eyes shall be opened, and ye shall be as gods, knowing good and evil. 6And when the woman saw that the tree was good for food, and that it was pleasant to the eyes, and a tree to be desired to make one wise, she took of the fruit thereof, and did eat, and gave also unto her husband with her; and he did eat. 7And the eyes of them both were opened, and they knew that they were naked; and they sewed fig leaves together, and made themselves aprons.

THE CREATION OF MAN AND WOMAN IN GOD'S IMAGE: GENESIS 1:24-31.

24And God said, Let the earth bring forth the living creature after his kind, cattle, and creeping thing, and beast of the earth after his kind: and it was so. 25And God made the beast of the earth after his kind, and cattle after their kind, and every thing that creepeth upon the earth after his kind: and God saw that it was good. 26And God said, Let us make man in our image, after our likeness: and let them have dominion over the fish of the sea, and over the fowl of the air, and over the cattle, and over all the earth, and over every creeping thing that creepeth upon the earth. <u>27So God created man in his own image, in the image of God created he him; male and female created he</u>

them. 28And God blessed them, and God said unto them, Be fruitful, and multiply, and replenish the earth, and subdue it: and have dominion over the fish of the sea, and over the fowl of the air, and over every living thing that moveth upon the earth. 29And God said, Behold, I have given you every herb bearing seed, which is upon the face of all the earth, and every tree, in the which is the fruit of a tree yielding seed; to you it shall be for meat. 30And to every beast of the earth, and to every fowl of the air, and to every thing that creepeth upon the earth, wherein there is life, I have given every green herb for meat: and it was so. 31And God saw every thing that he had made, and, behold, it was very good. And the evening and the morning were the sixth day.

THE "ONE-FLESH" PARADIGM: GENESIS 2:7-25.

7And the LORD God formed man of the dust of the ground, and breathed into his nostrils the breath of life; and man became a living soul. 8And the LORD God planted a garden eastward in Eden; and there he put the man whom he had formed. 9And out of the ground made the LORD God to grow every tree that is pleasant to the sight, and good for food; the tree of life also in the midst of the garden, and the tree of knowledge of good and evil. 10And a river went out of Eden to water the garden; and from thence it was parted, and became into four heads. 11The name of the first is Pison: that is it which compasseth the whole land of Havilah, where there is gold; 12And the gold of that land is good: there is bdellium and the onyx stone.

13And the name of the second river is Gihon: the same is it that compasseth the whole land of Ethiopia. 14And the name of the third river is Hiddekel: that is it which goeth toward the east of Assyria. And the fourth river is Euphrates. 15And the LORD God took the man, and put him into the garden of Eden to dress it and to keep it. 16And the LORD God commanded the man, saying, Of every tree of the garden thou mayest freely eat: 17But of the tree of the knowledge of good and evil, thou shalt not eat of it: for in the day that thou eatest thereof thou shalt surely die. 18And the LORD God said, It is not good that the man should be alone; I will make him an help meet for him. 19And out of the ground the LORD God formed every beast of the field, and every fowl of the air; and brought them unto Adam to see what he would call them: and whatsoever Adam called every living creature, that was the name thereof. 20And Adam gave names to all cattle, and to the fowl of the air, and to every beast of the field; but for Adam there was not found an help meet for him. 21And the LORD God caused a deep sleep to fall upon Adam, and he slept: and he took one of his ribs, and closed up the flesh instead thereof; 22And the rib, which the LORD God had taken from man, made he a woman, and brought her unto the man. 23And Adam said, This is now bone of my bones, and flesh of my flesh: she shall be called Woman, because she was taken out of Man. 24<u>Therefore shall a man leave his father and his mother, and shall cleave unto his wife: and they shall be one flesh.</u> 25And they were both naked, the man and his wife, and were not ashamed.

WICKEDNESS IN THE DAYS OF NOAH: GENESIS 6:1-12

1And it came to pass, when men began to multiply on the face of the earth, and daughters were born unto them, 2That the sons of God saw the daughters of men that they were fair; and they took them wives of all which they chose. 3And the LORD said, My spirit shall not always strive with man, for that he also is flesh: yet his days shall be an hundred and twenty years. 4There were giants in the earth in those days; and also after that, when the sons of God came in unto the daughters of men, and they bare children to them, the same became mighty men which were of old, men of renown. 5<u>And GOD saw that the wickedness of man was great in the earth, and that every imagination of the thoughts of his heart was only evil continually.</u> 6And it repented the LORD that he had made man on the earth, and it grieved him at his heart. 7And the LORD said, I will destroy man whom I have created from the face of the earth; both man, and beast, and the creeping thing, and the fowls of the air; for it repenteth me that I have made them. 8But Noah found grace in the eyes of the LORD. 9These are the generations of Noah: Noah was a just man and perfect in his generations, and Noah walked with God. 10And Noah begat three sons, Shem, Ham, and Japheth. 11The earth also was corrupt before God, and the earth was filled with violence. 12<u>And God looked upon the earth, and, behold, it was corrupt; for all flesh had corrupted his way upon the earth.</u>

THE RAINBOW AS GOD'S SYMBOL OF HIS PRESENCE AND AUTHORITY: GENESIS 9:8-17.

8And God spake unto Noah, and to his sons with him, saying, 9And I, behold, I establish my covenant with you, and with your seed after you; 10And with every living creature that is with you, of the fowl, of the cattle, and of every beast of the earth with you; from all that go out of the ark, to every beast of the earth. 11And I will establish my covenant with you; neither shall all flesh be cut off any more by the waters of a flood; neither shall there any more be a flood to destroy the earth. <u>12And God said, This is the token of the covenant which I make between me and you and every living creature that is with you, for perpetual generations: 13I do set my bow in the cloud, and it shall be for a token of a covenant between me and the earth. 14And it shall come to pass, when I bring a cloud over the earth, that the bow shall be seen in the cloud: 15And I will remember my covenant, which is between me and you and every living creature of all flesh; and the waters shall no more become a flood to destroy all flesh. 16And the bow shall be in the cloud; and I will look upon it, that I may remember the everlasting covenant between God and every living creature of all flesh that is upon the earth. 17And God said unto Noah, This is the token of the covenant, which I have established between me and all flesh that is upon the earth.</u>

THE SEXUAL PERVERSION OF NOAH'S GRANDSON CANAAN: GENESIS 9:20-25.

20And Noah began to be an husbandman, and he planted a vineyard: 21And he drank of the wine, and was drunken; and he was uncovered within his tent. <u>22And Ham, the father of Canaan, saw the nakedness of his father</u>, and told his two brethren without. 23And Shem and Japheth took a garment, and laid it upon both their shoulders, and went backward, and covered the nakedness of their father; and their faces were backward, and they saw not their father's nakedness. <u>24And Noah awoke from his wine, and knew what his younger son had done unto him. 25And he said, Cursed be Canaan</u>; a servant of servants shall he be unto his brethren.

THE NATURE OF CANAAN'S PERVERSION AND THE MEANING OF "NAKEDNESS:" LEVITICUS 18:6-7; 20:11.

6None of you shall approach to any that is near of kin to him, to uncover their nakedness: I am the LORD. <u>7The nakedness of thy father, or the nakedness of thy mother, shalt thou not uncover</u>: she is thy mother; thou shalt not uncover her nakedness.

<u>11And the man that lieth with his father's wife hath uncovered his father's nakedness</u>: both of them shall surely be put to death; their blood shall be upon them.

THE SIN OF SODOM: GENESIS 19:1-27.

1And there came two angels to Sodom at even; and Lot sat in the gate of Sodom: and Lot seeing them rose up to meet them; and he bowed himself with his face toward the ground; 2And he said, Behold now, my lords, turn in, I pray you, into your servant's house, and tarry all night, and wash your feet, and ye shall rise up early, and go on your ways. And they said, Nay; but we will abide in the street all night. 3And he pressed upon them greatly; and they turned in unto him, and entered into his house; and he made them a feast, and did bake unleavened bread, and they did eat. 4<u>But before they lay down, the men of the city, even the men of Sodom, compassed the house round, both old and young, all the people from every quarter: 5And they called unto Lot, and said unto him, Where are the men which came in to thee this night? bring them out unto us, that we may know them.</u> 6And Lot went out at the door unto them, and shut the door after him, 7And said, I pray you, brethren, do not so wickedly. 8Behold now, I have two daughters which have not known man; let me, I pray you, bring them out unto you, and do ye to them as is good in your eyes: only unto these men do nothing; for therefore came they under the shadow of my roof. 9And they said, Stand back. And they said again, This one fellow came in to sojourn, and he will needs be a judge: now will we deal worse with thee, than with them. And they pressed sore upon the man, even Lot, and came near to break the door. 10But the men put forth their hand, and pulled Lot into the house to them, and shut to the door. 11And they smote the men that were at the door of the house with blindness, both small and great: so that they wearied themselves to find the door. 12And the men said unto Lot, Hast thou here any besides? son in law, and thy sons, and thy daughters, and whatsoever thou hast in the city, bring them out of this place: 13For we will destroy this place, because the cry of them is waxen great before the face of the LORD; and the LORD hath sent us to destroy it. 14And Lot went out, and spake unto his sons in law, which married his daughters, and said, Up, get you out of this place; for the LORD will destroy this city. But he seemed as one that mocked unto his sons in law. 15And when the morning arose, then the angels hastened Lot, saying, Arise, take thy wife, and thy two daughters, which are here; lest thou be consumed in the iniquity of the city. 16And while he lingered, the men laid hold upon his hand, and upon the hand of his wife, and upon the hand of his two daughters; the LORD being merciful unto him: and they brought him forth, and set him without the city. 17And it came to pass, when they had brought them forth abroad, that he said, Escape for thy life; look not behind thee, neither stay thou in all the plain; escape to the mountain, lest thou be consumed. 18And Lot said unto them, Oh, not so, my Lord: 19Behold now, thy servant hath found grace in thy sight, and thou hast magnified thy mercy, which thou hast shewed unto me in saving my life; and I cannot escape to the mountain, lest some evil take me, and I die: 20Behold now, this city is near to flee unto, and it is a little one: Oh, let me escape thither, (is it not a little one?) and my soul shall live. 21And he said unto him, See, I have accepted thee concerning this thing also, that I will not overthrow this city, for the which thou hast spoken. 22Haste thee, escape thither; for I cannot do any thing till thou be come thither. Therefore the name of the city was called Zoar. 23The sun was risen upon the earth when Lot entered into Zoar. **24Then the LORD rained upon Sodom and upon Gomorrah brimstone and fire from the LORD out of heaven; 25And he overthrew those cities, and all the plain, and all the inhabitants of the cities, and that which grew upon the ground.** 26But his wife looked back from behind him, and she became a pillar of salt. 27And Abraham gat up early in the morning to the place where he stood before the LORD: 28And he looked toward Sodom and Gomorrah, and toward all the land of the plain, and beheld, and, lo, the smoke of the country went up as the smoke of a furnace.

THE SEXUAL PERVERSIONS THAT DEFINED CANAANITE IDOLATRY: LEVITICUS 18:1-30.

1And the LORD spake unto Moses, saying, 2Speak unto the children of Israel, and say unto them, I am the LORD your God. 3After the doings of the land of Egypt, wherein ye dwelt, shall ye not do: and after the doings of the land of Canaan, whither I bring you, shall ye not do: neither shall ye walk in their ordinances. 4Ye shall do my judgments, and keep mine ordinances, to walk therein: I am the LORD your God. 5Ye shall therefore keep my statutes, and my judgments: which if a man do, he shall live in them: I am the LORD. 6None of you shall approach to any that is near of kin to him, to uncover their nakedness: I am the LORD. 7The nakedness of thy father, or the nakedness of thy mother, shalt thou not uncover: she is thy mother; thou shalt not uncover her nakedness. 8The nakedness of thy father's wife shalt thou not uncover: it is thy father's nakedness. 9The nakedness of thy sister, the daughter of thy father, or daughter of thy mother, whether she be born at home, or born abroad, even their nakedness thou shalt not uncover. 10The nakedness of thy son's daughter, or of thy daughter's daughter, even their nakedness thou shalt not uncover: for theirs is thine own nakedness. 11The nakedness of thy father's wife's daughter, begotten of thy father, she is thy sister, thou shalt not uncover her nakedness. 12Thou shalt not uncover the nakedness of thy father's sister: she is thy father's near kinswoman. 13Thou shalt not uncover the nakedness of thy mother's sister: for she is thy mother's near kinswoman. 14Thou shalt not uncover the nakedness of thy father's brother, thou shalt not approach to his wife: she is thine aunt. 15Thou shalt not uncover the nakedness of thy daughter in law: she is thy son's wife; thou shalt not uncover her nakedness. 16Thou shalt not uncover the nakedness of thy brother's wife: it is thy brother's nakedness. 17Thou shalt not uncover the nakedness of a woman and her daughter, neither shalt thou take her son's daughter, or her daughter's daughter, to uncover her nakedness; for they are her near kinswomen: it is wickedness. 18Neither shalt thou take a wife to her sister, to vex her, to uncover her nakedness, beside the other in her life time. 19Also thou shalt not approach unto a woman to uncover her nakedness, as long as she is put apart for her uncleanness. 20Moreover thou shalt not lie carnally with thy neighbour's wife, to defile thyself with her. 21And thou shalt not let any of thy seed pass through the fire to Molech, neither shalt thou profane the name of thy God: I am the LORD. 22<u>Thou shalt not lie with mankind, as with womankind: it is abomination.</u> 23<u>Neither shalt thou lie with any beast to</u>

defile thyself therewith: neither shall any woman stand before a beast to lie down thereto: it is confusion. 24Defile not ye yourselves in any of these things: for in all these the nations are defiled which I cast out before you: 25And the land is defiled: therefore I do visit the iniquity thereof upon it, and the land itself vomiteth out her inhabitants. 26Ye shall therefore keep my statutes and my judgments, and shall not commit any of these abominations; neither any of your own nation, nor any stranger that sojourneth among you: 27(For all these abominations have the men of the land done, which were before you, and the land is defiled;) 28That the land spue not you out also, when ye defile it, as it spued out the nations that were before you. 29For whosoever shall commit any of these abominations, even the souls that commit them shall be cut off from among their people. 30Therefore shall ye keep mine ordinance, that ye commit not any one of these abominable customs, which were committed before you, and that ye defile not yourselves therein: I am the LORD your God.

THE SECOND SODOM – TRIGGERING CIVIL WAR AMONG THE HEBREW TRIBES: JUDGES 19:1-30.

1And it came to pass in those days, when there was no king in Israel, that there was a certain Levite sojourning on the side of mount Ephraim, who took to him a concubine out of Bethlehemjudah. 2And his concubine played the whore against him, and went away from him unto her father's house to Bethlehemjudah, and was there four whole months. 3And her husband arose, and went after her, to speak friendly unto her, and to bring her again, having his servant with him, and a couple of asses: and she brought him into her father's house: and when the father of the damsel saw him, he rejoiced to meet him. 4And his father in law, the damsel's father, retained him; and he abode with him three days: so they did eat and drink, and lodged there. 5And it came to pass on the fourth day, when they arose early in the morning, that he rose up to depart: and the damsel's father said unto his son in law, Comfort thine heart with a morsel of bread, and afterward go your way. 6And they sat down, and did eat and drink both of them together: for the damsel's father had said unto the man, Be content, I pray thee, and tarry all night, and let thine heart be merry. 7And when the man rose up to depart, his father in law urged him: therefore he lodged there again. 8And he arose early in the morning on the fifth day to depart: and the damsel's father said, Comfort thine heart, I pray thee. And they tarried until afternoon, and they did eat both of them. 9And when the man rose up to depart, he, and his concubine, and his servant, his father in law, the damsel's father, said unto him, Behold, now the day draweth toward evening, I pray you tarry all night: behold, the day groweth to an end, lodge here, that thine heart may be merry; and to morrow get you early on your way, that thou mayest go home. 10But the man would not tarry that night, but he rose up and departed, and came over against Jebus, which is Jerusalem; and there were with him two asses saddled, his concubine also was with him. 11And when they were by Jebus, the day was far spent; and the servant said unto his master, Come, I pray thee, and let us turn in into this city of the Jebusites, and lodge in it. 12And his master said unto him, We will not turn aside hither into the city of a stranger, that is not of the children of Israel; we will pass over to Gibeah. 13And he said unto his servant, Come, and let us draw near to one of these places to lodge all night, in Gibeah, or in Ramah. 14And they passed on and went their way; and the sun went down upon them when they were by Gibeah, which belongeth to Benjamin. 15And they turned aside thither, to go in and to lodge in Gibeah: and when he went in, he sat him down in a street of the city: for there was no man that took them into his house to lodging. 16And, behold, there came an old man from his work out of the field at even, which was also of mount Ephraim; and he sojourned in Gibeah: but the men of the place were Benjamites. 17And when he had lifted up his eyes, he saw a wayfaring man in the street of the city: and the old man said, Whither goest thou? and whence comest thou? 18And he said unto him, We are passing from Bethlehemjudah toward the side of mount Ephraim; from thence am I: and I went to Bethlehemjudah, but I am now going to the house of the LORD; and there is no man that receiveth me to house. 19Yet there is both straw and provender for our asses; and there is bread and wine also for me, and for thy handmaid, and for the young man which is with thy servants: there is no want of any thing. <u>20And the old man said, Peace be with thee; howsoever let all thy wants lie upon me; only lodge not in the street.</u> 21So he brought him into his house, and gave provender unto the asses: and they washed their feet, and did eat and drink. <u>22Now as they were making their hearts merry, behold, the men of the city, certain sons of Belial, beset the house round about, and beat at the door, and spake to the master of the house, the old man, saying, Bring forth the man that came</u>

<u>into thine house, that we may know him. 23And the man, the master of the house, went out unto them, and said unto them, Nay, my brethren, nay, I pray you, do not so wickedly; seeing that this man is come into mine house, do not this folly. 24Behold, here is my daughter a maiden, and his concubine; them I will bring out now, and humble ye them, and do with them what seemeth good unto you: but unto this man do not so vile a thing. 25But the men would not hearken to him: so the man took his concubine, and brought her forth unto them; and they knew her, and abused her all the night until the morning: and when the day began to spring, they let her go.</u> 26Then came the woman in the dawning of the day, and fell down at the door of the man's house where her lord was, till it was light. 27And her lord rose up in the morning, and opened the doors of the house, and went out to go his way: and, behold, the woman his concubine was fallen down at the door of the house, and her hands were upon the threshold. 28And he said unto her, Up, and let us be going. But none answered. Then the man took her up upon an ass, and the man rose up, and gat him unto his place. 29And when he was come into his house, he took a knife, and laid hold on his concubine, and divided her, together with her bones, into twelve pieces, and sent her into all the coasts of Israel. 30And it was so, that all that saw it said, There was no such deed done nor seen from the day that the children of Israel came up out of the land of Egypt unto this day: consider of it, take advice, and speak your minds.

THE NEW TESTAMENT REPEATS THE CONDEMNATION OF HOMOSEXUAL SIN AND IDENTIFIES IT WITH THE REPROBATE MIND AND CULTURE OF APOSTASY: ROMANS 1:18-32

18For the wrath of God is revealed from heaven against all ungodliness and unrighteousness of men, who hold the truth in unrighteousness; 19Because that which may be known of God is manifest in them; for God hath shewed it unto them. 20For the invisible things of him from the creation of the world are clearly seen, being understood by the things that are made, even his eternal power and Godhead; so that they are without excuse: 21Because that, when they knew God, they glorified him not as God, neither were thankful; but became vain in their imaginations, and their foolish heart was darkened. 22Professing themselves to be wise, they became fools, 23And changed the glory of the uncorruptible God into an image made like to corruptible man, and to birds, and fourfooted beasts, and creeping things. 24Wherefore God also gave them up to uncleanness through the lusts of their own hearts, to dishonour their own bodies between themselves: 25Who changed the truth of God into a lie, and worshipped and served the creature more than the Creator, who is blessed for ever. Amen. <u>26For this cause God gave them up unto vile affections: for even their women did change the natural use into that which is against nature: 27And likewise also the men, leaving the natural use of the woman, burned in their lust one toward another; men with men working that which is unseemly, and receiving in themselves that recompence of their error which was meet.</u> 28And even as they did not like to retain God in their knowledge, God gave them over to a reprobate mind, to do those things which are not convenient; 29Being filled with all unrighteousness, fornication, wickedness, covetousness, maliciousness; full of envy, murder, debate, deceit, malignity; whisperers, 30Backbiters, haters of God, despiteful, proud, boasters, inventors of evil things, disobedient to parents, 31Without understanding, covenantbreakers, without natural affection, implacable, unmerciful: 32Who knowing the judgment of God, that they which commit such things are worthy of death, not only do the same, but have pleasure in them that do them.

ALL HOMOSEXUALS CAN BE HEALED BY CHRIST AS SOME WERE IN THE EARLY CHURCH: 1 CORINTHIANS 6:2-11.

2Do ye not know that the saints shall judge the world? and if the world shall be judged by you, are ye unworthy to judge the smallest matters? 3Know ye not that we shall judge angels? how much more things that pertain to this life? 4If then ye have judgments of things pertaining to this life, set them to judge who are least esteemed in the church. 5I speak to your shame. Is it so, that there is not a wise man among you? no, not one that shall be able to judge between his brethren? 6But brother goeth to law with brother, and that before the unbelievers. 7Now therefore there is utterly a fault among you, because ye go to law one with another. Why do ye not rather take wrong? why do ye not rather suffer yourselves to be defrauded? 8Nay, ye do wrong, and defraud, and that your brethren. 9<u>Know ye not that the unrighteous shall not inherit the</u>

kingdom of God? Be not deceived: neither fornicators, nor idolaters, nor adulterers, nor effeminate, nor abusers of themselves with mankind, 10Nor thieves, nor covetous, nor drunkards, nor revilers, nor extortioners, shall inherit the kingdom of God. 11And such were some of you: but ye are washed, but ye are sanctified, but ye are justified in the name of the Lord Jesus, and by the Spirit of our God.

HOMOSEXUAL SIN IS LAWLESSNESS EQUIVALENT TO MURDER AND KIDNAPPING: 1 TIMOTHY 1:8-10.

8But we know that the law is good, if a man use it lawfully; 9Knowing this, that the law is not made for a righteous man, but for the lawless and disobedient, for the ungodly and for sinners, for unholy and profane, for murderers of fathers and murderers of mothers, for manslayers, 10For whoremongers, for them that defile themselves with mankind, for menstealers, for liars, for perjured persons, and if there be any other thing that is contrary to sound doctrine; 11According to the glorious gospel of the blessed God, which was committed to my trust.

SODOM'S DESTRUCTION HOMOSEXUALITY IS FORETASTE OF THE FINAL JUDGMENT BY FIRE: JUDE 1:5-8.

5I will therefore put you in remembrance, though ye once knew this, how that the Lord, having saved the people out of the land of Egypt, afterward destroyed them that believed not. 6And the angels which kept not their first estate, but left their own habitation, he hath reserved in everlasting chains under darkness unto the judgment of the great day. 7<u>Even as Sodom and Gomorrha, and the cities about them in like manner, giving themselves over to fornication, and going after strange flesh, are set forth for an example, suffering the vengeance of eternal fire.</u> 8Likewise also these filthy dreamers defile the flesh, despise dominion, and speak evil of dignities.

THE PROPHECY OF SIMON PETER OF A LAST DAYS HERESY: 2 PETER 2.

1<u>But there were false prophets also among the people, even as there shall be false teachers among you, who privily shall bring in damnable heresies, even denying the Lord that bought them, and bring upon themselves swift destruction. 2And many shall follow their pernicious ways; by reason of whom the way of truth shall be evil spoken of.</u> 3And through covetousness shall they with feigned words make merchandise of you: whose judgment now of a long time lingereth not, and their damnation slumbereth not. 4For if God spared not the angels that sinned, but cast them down to hell, and delivered them into chains of darkness, to be reserved unto judgment; 5And spared not the old world, but saved Noah the eighth person, a preacher of righteousness, bringing in the flood upon the world of the ungodly; 6<u>And turning the cities of Sodom and Gomorrha into ashes condemned them with an overthrow, making them an ensample unto those that after should live</u>

ungodly; 7And delivered just Lot, vexed with the filthy conversation of the wicked: 8(For that righteous man dwelling among them, in seeing and hearing, vexed his righteous soul from day to day with their unlawful deeds;) 9The Lord knoweth how to deliver the godly out of temptations, and to reserve the unjust unto the day of judgment to be punished: 10But chiefly them that walk after the flesh in the lust of uncleanness, and despise government. Presumptuous are they, selfwilled, they are not afraid to speak evil of dignities. 11Whereas angels, which are greater in power and might, bring not railing accusation against them before the Lord. 12But these, as natural brute beasts, made to be taken and destroyed, speak evil of the things that they understand not; and shall utterly perish in their own corruption; 13And shall receive the reward of unrighteousness, as they that count it pleasure to riot in the day time. Spots they are and blemishes, sporting themselves with their own deceivings while they feast with you; 14Having eyes full of adultery, and that cannot cease from sin; beguiling unstable souls: an heart they have exercised with covetous practices; cursed children: 15Which have forsaken the right way, and are gone astray, following the way of Balaam the son of Bosor, who loved the wages of unrighteousness; 16But was rebuked for his iniquity: the dumb ass speaking with man's voice forbad the madness of the prophet. 17These are wells without water, clouds that are carried with a tempest; to whom the mist of darkness is reserved for ever. 18 For when they speak great swelling words of vanity, they allure through the lusts of the flesh, through much wantonness, those that were clean escaped from them who live in error. 19While they promise them liberty, they themselves are the

<u>servants of corruption: for of whom a man is overcome, of the same is he brought in bondage.</u> 20For if after they have escaped the pollutions of the world through the knowledge of the Lord and Saviour Jesus Christ, they are again entangled therein, and overcome, the latter end is worse with them than the beginning. 21For it had been better for them not to have known the way of righteousness, than, after they have known it, to turn from the holy commandment delivered unto them. 22But it is happened unto them according to the true proverb, The dog is turned to his own vomit again; and the sow that was washed to her wallowing in the mire.

THE KINGDOM OF THE ANTICHRIST IS DEFINED IN PART BY HOMOSEXUALITY: REVELATION 11:7-9.

7And when they shall have finished their testimony, the beast that ascendeth out of the bottomless pit shall make war against them, and shall overcome them, and kill them. <u>8And their dead bodies shall lie in the street of the great city, which spiritually is called Sodom and Egypt, where also our Lord was crucified.</u> 9And they of the people and kindreds and tongues and nations shall see their dead bodies three days and an half, and shall not suffer their dead bodies to be put in graves.

Appendix B:

Six Prophetic Essays Regarding "Gay Theology" by Dr. Scott Lively

The following articles are presented just as they were written and posted at Dr. Lively's blog, www.scottlively.net. They contain numerous facts and analysis that are repeated in the text of this book and show the evolution of his understanding and arguments on the topic of "gay theology." They also address aspects of the issue and current events outside the scope of this book that may be of interest to the reader.

THE PETROS PROPHECY: SIMON PETER'S WARNING ABOUT THE HERESY OF THE LAST DAYS

A WARNING TO THE CHURCH IN AMERICA

Article written June 13, 2013. Preface written June 23, 2013, when the article was published.

Preface:

I have hesitated about publishing this article because its tone is so dire and so few in the church are ready to receive it. However, just a few days after I wrote it Alan Chambers shut down Exodus International and publicly announced his embrace of the same "gay" theology I warn about in the article. I have taken that as a sign I should release this now.

In a few days the Supreme Court will announce it's ruling on at least one of the homosexual cases now before it. I'm predicting that we'll lose at least one of them, probably both, and my guess is the results will be announced on Friday June 28th. That is "Gay Pride Day," the anniversary of the Stonewall riots in which the homosexual movement shifted its goal from "the right to be left alone," to absolute control of American culture. It was the birth of homofascism in this nation. If the latter prediction comes true it will be an indication that SCOTUS is now under their control. It will be the symbolic equivalent to the lowering of the American flag and replacement with the rainbow flag. (It is possible, though not likely, they will actually fly the rainbow flag at the court on that day. They do so love to gloat.)

However, the warning below applies even if we win both cases! The only question is how fast their army will move against us. If we lose one or both cases it will be "pedal to the metal" just like the drive for "gay marriage" after *Lawrence v Texas.*

If we do win one of the cases, my guess it will be DOMA. I think Justice Gindberg's comments last month about *Roe v Wade* having been a bad ruling because the country wasn't quite ready for it may have been to telegraph a message to the leftist elite that the court was not going to strike down DOMA. We'll soon see.

One last comment. In my reading of the Bible these things must take place before the return of the Lord, so I am not discouraged but encouraged. Like a woman going into labor I'm looking past the pain to the blessing that follows.

Article:

You may have heard of me. I am the pastor being sued in U.S. Federal Court for "Crimes Against Humanity" for preaching against homosexuality in Uganda. But I am really a "Canary in the Coal Mine," with a warning for every Bible-believing Christian in our land, especially pastors and ministry leaders.

The American church is about to come under spiritual and cultural warfare the likes of which we have never seen and which most are not prepared for. The attacks will come from every corner of the secular world to challenge, condemn and punish us for our beliefs about homosexuality. These attacks will split denominations, congregations and even Christian families to a degree and with an intensity that will shock even those who have experienced the first ripples of "gay" conflict in the church over the past few decades.

Large numbers of self-identified Christians will begin embracing so-called "Gay Theology," and some will actually join the attacks against the remnant who stand firm on the truth. The pressure to give in to escape the psychological and sometimes physical persecution of the Christian "homophobes" will be so great that I believe a majority of church-goers will succumb, and a great many pastors will choose to "change with the times," so as not to lose "their" church.

This collapse of the Christian infrastructure of America is, in my opinion, already in progress and irreversible because it is part of God's judgment. The "end-times" revival which many, including myself, expect and eagerly await will not stop this collapse, but will in fact hasten it by strengthening the remnant in their obedience to Christ while hardening the world (and fallen Christians) against us. The crisis will be so pervasive that no-one will be spared the choice of embracing or rejecting Biblical truth on this topic. The whole purpose of this trial is to test the strength of believers to endure greater troubles ahead.

We shouldn't be surprised that God is using this issue as our test. A careful examination of His Word shows that open homosexuality in the Bible is symbolic of extreme rebellion against God leading to judgment. Thus, unique in all of scripture, Sodom and Gomorrah are destroyed by fire and brimstone as the examplar of God's wrath (2 Peter

2:6, Jude 1:7, Genesis 19:1-12), male on male sodomy is listed as the most heinous sin on the short list of sins which caused the land to "*vomit out*" the Canaanites from the territory promised to Abraham (Leviticus 18:1-30, esp. 22), and both male and female homosexuality are together identified as the examplar of the depraved or "reprobate" mind that defines the age of apostasy leading to Christ's return (Romans 1:18-32, 2 Timothy 3:1-5).

Noah's Flood was preceded by the "*marrying and giving in marriage*" (Matt 24:37-40) of people whose thoughts were "*only evil continually*" (Genesis 6:5), evidence which the ancient Hebrew scholars interpreted as "gay marriage," the final insult to God which unleashed the deluge. And in the final book of the Bible, just prior to the return of Christ to "*judge and make war*" against His enemies (Rev 19:11ff), Jerusalem under the Antichrist is "*mystically called Sodom and Egypt,*" signifying its essential association (I believe) with homosexuality and polytheism respectively (Revelation 11:3-8).

Even 1 Corinthians 6:9-11, the "ex-gay" passage that proves that healed and recovered homosexuals were a part of the church from its earliest days, warns that unrepentant homosexuals "*will not enter the Kingdom of Heaven.*" There is no room, even when we emphasize compassion for homosexual sufferers, to condone homosexual relationships or worse, to claim that homosexuality is blessed by God as a normal, intended variant of human sexuality.

My life's work has been to stand against the (increasingly successful) assault of the homosexual movement on

Biblical values in our society and around the world. My nearly 25 years of full time, front lines ministry on this battlefield has given me special insights and understanding of this issue. My refusal to be silenced by a long series of increasingly more dishonest and aggressive attacks on my work and reputation has familiarized me both with persecution and with the tactical "playbook" of the "gay" movement. I am thus issuing my warning to the church not so much as a prophesy (though it is confirmed in my spirit), but as the natural conclusion of deductive reasoning by a front-lines analyst with a unique vantage-point. In support of that conclusion, I offer the following observations.

First, on June 28, 1969 the goal of the American homosexual movement shifted from tolerance (the right to be left alone) to control (the complete restructuring of society in its own image, with "gays" or their surrogates in all seats of power). Its tactics shifted from civil dialogue to implacable militancy. That was the date of the Stonewall Riot in New York City, today celebrated annually as "Gay Pride Day." Logically, this movement cannot achieve its goal without replacing the Biblical social ethic of marriage-based heterosexual monogamy and the natural family with its own philosophy of unlimited "sexual freedom" (which is in reality moral anarchy). In short, the true and necessary goal of the "gay" movement is the defeat of Christianity.

Second, in the space of just forty years homosexual militants have defeated every secular institution in their path in the United States. The first to fall was the American Psychiatric Association in 1973, when "gay" activists, using

Brownshirt tactics of disruption and intimidation, forced the APA to remove homosexuality from its list of mental disorders in its *Diagnostic and Statistical Manual IV*. The most recent and final secular institution to fall was the Boy Scouts of America in 2013 when the BSA leadership voted to allow openly self-declared homosexual boys into the organization. The next-to-last entity to fall was the U. S. military. In both cases, the first news following the capitulation was of uniformed members of each organization marching triumphantly in "Gay Pride" parades.

Third, the "gays" have always intended to attack the church in the final stage of their conquest of our culture. As early as 1987 they openly admitted this plan in an article called "The Overhauling of Straight America," which later became the basis for the book *After the Ball*, which has ever since been their primary strategic blueprint. They wrote:

When conservative churches condemn gays...we can use talk to muddy the moral waters. This means publicizing support for gays by more moderate churches, raising theological objections of our own about conservative interpretations of biblical teachings, and exposing hatred and inconsistency. Second, we can undermine the moral authority of homophobic churches by portraying them as antiquated backwaters, badly out of step with the times and with the latest findings of psychology. Against the mighty pull of institutional Religion one must set the mightier draw of Science & Public Opinion (the shield and sword of that accursed "secular humanism"). Such an unholy alliance has worked well against churches before, on such topics as divorce and abortion. .... At a later stage...it will be time to get tough with remaining opponents. To be blunt, they must be vilified. (*Guide Magazine*, November 1987)

Frankly, even at this late stage of the game, much of the church seems to be still asleep or in denial about the state of our culture. Even many conservative Christian leaders who are awake to the seriousness of the crisis are only dimly aware that the culture war at its foundation is and has always been a winner-take-all contest between Christians and homosexual activists. Now that the last secular barriers to the "gay" agenda have been crushed, all of their weapons and all of their warriors will be focused on the last remaining obstacle to their power, the Christian church.

What comes next is a full-on homosexual blitzkrieg against "homophobia" and "hatred" in the church, and a concurrent culture-wide advocacy of "gay theology." Gone, of course, will be all concern for the "separation of church and state" as the secular powers work hand-in-hand with the "gays" to shame and "correct" the Bible-believing church, using Scripture that has been deviously twisted to fit their goals. The only defense will be Biblical literacy backed by unshakable faith. To be blunt, we will be all be vilified and only the strong of faith will endure.

To be sure, one's view of homosexuality is not necessarily a salvation issue, but one's ability to cling to Christ through persecution may well be. Will a person too spiritually weak or cowardly to defend Biblical truth on such a clear and fundamental teaching be strong enough to resist the Mark of the Beast? During a time of testing such as we are entering, the Prophet Jeremiah put it this way: "*If you have run with footmen and they have tired you out, Then how can you compete with horses? If you fall down in a land of peace, How will you do in the thicket of the Jordan?*"

It might not be noticeable now, but their campaign has been launched and will steadily increase in breadth, depth and persuasiveness. Remnant, be prepared, and share this warning.

###

CHURCH WARNING UPDATE

Written July 2, 2013

The country is still reeling from the recent Supreme Court "marriage" rulings. I am not happy to have been right in my predictions that we would lose at least one, but probably both cases, and that Justice Kennedy would write the majority opinion to reflect his personal goal to legitimize homosexuality in America. He did so in the DOMA case *United States. v. Windsor.* The Proposition 8 case, *Hollingsworth v Perry* was remanded back to the lower court where there was technically another opportunity to defend it in court.

However, in my newsletter I opined that Prop 8 was as good as dead and told people to watch for dirty tricks and sabotage to circumvent due process. Sure enough, the Ninth Circuit Appeals court announced the following day they would move immediately to allow the resumption of "gay marriages." Prop 8 attorney Andy Pugno was outraged, writing

"Suspiciously, the Ninth Circuit's announcement late Friday ordering same-sex marriages came as a surprise, without any warning or notice to Proposition 8's official proponents. However, the same-sex couple plaintiffs in the case, their media teams, San Francisco City Hall, L.A. Mayor Antonio Villaraigosa and the California Attorney General all happened to be in position to perform same-sex marriages just minutes after the Ninth Circuit's "unexpected" announcement. Coincidence?"

His emergency petition to the Supreme Court was instantly rejected by Justice Kennedy (whom Don Feder has aptly named "Ronald Reagan's most tragic mistake"). So California has now officially fallen.

But this sort of lawlessness is simply par for the course whenever the sacred cow of homosexuality is at issue. As Mat Staver of Liberty Counsel noted in the Winsor decision: "The decision is as far removed from the Constitution and the Court's prior precedent as the east is from the west. Led by Justice Kennedy, the majority of the Justices have cut the tether that once connected them to the Constitution. This decision does not even pretend to be governed by the Constitution or Court precedent." To me this is just one more indicator that the rising black fog of homofascism is an end-times spiritual phenomenon.

In a previous post I had suggested that Justice Ginsberg had been (on behalf of the liberal block) telegraphing a message to the leftist elite when she made public comments criticizing *Roe v Wade* for getting too far ahead of the public on the abortion issue and creating a "militant" backlash (the pro-life movement). I thought her comments meant they would vote to uphold DOMA. In fact, they instead voted to strike down DOMA, but NOT to recognize a constitutional right to homosexual marriage nationally, which the "gays" had asked and hoped for. Now we know what she meant.

So, while the *Winsor* decision clearly lays the groundwork for that next step, it seems the court will not take that step until the liberals believe the pubic will acquiesce to it peacefully. That bodes well for the pro-family movement

IF we can reverse the current "pro-gay" trend. But that's a very big IF. See my article, "The Key to Pro-Family Victory if We Really Want It:"

http://www.scottlively.net/2013/02/21/the-key-to-pro-family-victory-if-we-really-want-it/

Meanwhile, the homosexual propaganda machinery has been running at full capacity to create the impression in the public mind that they have won the culture war and all further resistance is futile. "Put down your weapons and run away," is their message to pro-family activists. And that message is being bolstered by their allies in the lower courts, the media and the political realm who are taking quick action to keep their momentum rolling.

A federal judge just ordered the State of Michigan to give financial benefits to homosexual partners. And it was just announced that Senator John McCain's political guru Steve Schmidt has been recruited by the ACLU to promote "gay marriage" in the GOP, see "ACLU launches campaign to win GOP support for gay marriage" at

http://dailycaller.com/2013/06/26/aclu-launches-campaign-to-win-gop-support-for-gay-marriage/#ixzz2XtnvIqqY

(which the Republican establishment obviously want to happen). Goodbye Whigs. Hello Tea Party.

But resistance is NOT futile and we must never surrender to evil. As Winston Churchill said:

"Still, if you will not fight for the right when you can easily win without bloodshed, if you will not fight when your victory will be sure and not so costly, you may come to the moment when you will have to fight with all the odds against you and only a precarious chance for survival. There may be a worse case. You may have to fight when there is no chance of victory, because it is better to perish than to live as slaves."

I believe we may be still at the cusp of the third and fourth stages, but more probably are at the fourth and final stage, Churchill's last stand.

I personally will never stop fighting to defend Biblical truth as long as I have breath. And I will fight to win every battle the Lord puts in my path, even when I perceive that winning that particular battle is impossible. The outcome of the "war," however is pre-determined by the Lord, and we know from His Word that ultimate victory will be by His hand at the very end after very dark days.

Today I am republishing my article A Warning to the Church in America because I want every pro-family activist in America to read it and circulate it to their pastor and to Christian friends. It is posted at my blog: www.scottlively.net.

Before you read that, let me suggest that our most effective tactic to resist the homosexual juggernaut is to amend all existing Sexual Orientation Regulations, wherever we may find them, with a First Amendment Supremacy Clause.

"Under no circumstance shall sexual orientation regulations supersede the First Amendment rights of individuals, churches and religious organizations to freedom of speech and freedom of religion. For the purpose of this amendment religious organizations are those whose policies or culture are substantially influenced by religious values including but not limited to Christian bookstores, adoption agencies, hospitals, non-profit and for- profit companies, social organizations and Christian student clubs on college campuses."

These First Amendment campaigns shift the focus of the debate to a contest between the First Amendment and Sexual Orientation Regulations, a battle we can win. I stand ready to assist you in any such effort.

I have just returned from a nine-stop speaking tour in Nebraska, which is now on-board with the First Amendment strategy, along with Oklahoma and Missouri. I am looking for more invitations to conservative states where we can put these in place as a roadblock to the homosexualization of those states and perhaps build some momentum in the other direction.

Let me also introduce the idea here that states with a state DOMA should use those statutes as a legal foundation and justification to create mandatory age-appropriate curricula for every grade level to educate the children about the meaning and importance of authentic marriage and how to prepare themselves for healthy and happy marriage in their own future. This will at the very least strengthen if not actually immunize many children from the influence of sexual anarchy and "gay" propaganda.   ###

THE PETROS PROPHECY: SIMON PETER'S WARNING ABOUT THE HERESY OF THE LAST DAYS

A LETTER TO THE INTERNATIONAL PRO-FAMILY MOVEMENT

Written December 31, 2015

I am Dr. Scott Lively, an attorney, pastor and President of Defend the Family International. For the past quarter century my ministry has been devoted to exposing and opposing the now-global homosexual movement, primarily in the United States, but with activity in more than thirty countries. I have been named public enemy number one by the world's largest homosexual organization, the Human Rights Campaign, labeled a "hate group" by the uber-leftist Southern Poverty Law Center, and targeted for personal destruction by the George Soros-funded Center For Constitutional Rights in a federal lawsuit (utilizing a team of fourteen lawyers), charging me with "Crimes Against Humanity" for preaching a reasoned, factual and non-violent message against homosexuality in Uganda.

I am in truth just a simple Christian missionary, running a one-man office with an annual budget of less than $120,000, but the enormously wealthy and powerful international homosexual network considers me one of it's greatest threats. Why? Because I know nearly as much about their history, strategies and tactics as they do and my life's work has been to empower and equip pro-family activists around the world with those facts.

Importantly, I have personally experienced or been an eyewitness to every form of harassment, intimidation and sabotage that homosexualists' employ to destroy anyone who dares to stand up to them. While I have known both male and female homosexuals who seemed like genuinely decent people despite being ensnared in sexual disoriention, I can confirm the warning of the Bible in Romans 1:24-32 that (in contrast) the leaders and activists of the LGBT movement are malicious deceivers and evil-doers, deliberately subverting civilized society and viciously attacking all opponents to advance their selfish and self-destructive interests.

I have paid a heavy price for the authority with which I speak, and I urge you to give credence to my testimony.

We must above all be honest with ourselves. With the **Obergefell v Hodges** so-called "gay marriage" decision of the United States Supreme Court, the American pro-family movement has been set back dramatically — to a position equivalent to that of the pro-life movement in 1973. Indeed, *Obergefell* is rightly described by many as the *Roe v Wade* of the homosexual issue, which fact has profound implications for us all.

My ministry is one of only a dozen or so single-issue pro-family organizations in the United States who speak the truth about homosexuality boldly and unapologetically, most of which are similarly small and not well funded. With a couple of exceptions, the larger multi-issue Christian conservative groups are shackled by fear of the politically-correct media and are unwilling to base their arguments on the abnormality of homosexuality itself, acquiescing to many key homosexual demands such as civil unions and sexual orientation regulations, thereby severely undermining their moral authority.

One by one, all of the influential secular institutions of the United States have capitulated to a decades-long campaign of homosexual bullying and to such a degree that today even the once staunchly conservative US Chamber of Commerce has become a tool of "gay" social engineering.

The American public education system (from pre-school through graduate school), our social media giants, and the majority of our news and entertainment media are not just pro-homosexual, but militantly so.

Our government is in the hands of a man called "The First Gay President" by *Newsweek* magazine (which intended it as a compliment), who has made the global advancement of homosexuality such a priority of his administration that over $700 million has been devoted to it in just the past three years.

Only the Christian church (and Torah-faithful Jews) continue to stand against the homosexual agenda in America and most of the western world. However, subjected as it is to constant, aggressive pro-"gay" advocacy and suppression of pro-family dissent in the popular culture and key institutions, the church is weakening, especially among its most vulnerable members, the youth.

That is the unfortunate reality not just in the United States, but the UK, Canada, the EU, and much of the rest of the western world.

Yet, though our situation is dire, even in the United States there remains work that can be done to reverse the current trend for those with long-term vision. And if we adopt a global perspective, and are willing to build international cooperation with morally-conservative countries (who still represent the vast majority of the world's population), there is realistic cause for optimism.

In my view as a veteran Christian missionary to the international pro-family movement there are three things we must do.

1. Inoculate the Church Against "Gay Theology"

First, we must protect and strengthen the Christian church by promoting Biblical literacy and fidelity regarding sexuality, marriage and family. Satan's greatest weapon against mankind has always been to sow doubt about God's Word and to present a plausible counterfeit alternative to those weak in faith and knowledge. The question, "Did God really say that?" was his trap in the Garden regarding the first sin, and it is his trap today regarding homosexuality. The more ignorant that Christians are of the Bible's stark warning about the personal and sociological dangers of homosexuality, the easier they are deceived.

For example, the now globally ubiquitous and seductive lie that homosexuality is innate and unchangeable, is directly and unmistakably refuted by 1 Corinthians 6:9-11, meaning that Christians who agree that "gays" are "born that way" and cannot change are literally denying Christ's authority and power, to their own spiritual peril.

Importantly, that lie is only one component of so-called "Gay Theology," a sophisticated and detailed revision of Biblical teachings on homosexuality in one unified and comprehensive package. Launched as a new variant of "gay" political propaganda in the 1980s by the openly homosexual historical revisionist John E Boswell of Yale University (who died in 1994 of AIDS), "Gay Theology" quickly evolved into a powerful tool of LGBT political activism and a central doctrine of numerous left-leaning Christian denominations. "Gay Theology" today represents the great heresy of our time and is advancing rapidly throughout the world, primarily among young people.

I have created a short pamphlet titled "NOT Just Another Sin" which outlines the Biblical case against homosexuality from Genesis to Revelation in a chronological series of bullet points. I expanded upon and explained how these references, when taken together, represent "The Forgotten Last Days Warning About Homosexuality in the Bible" in an 18-page article with that title. Both of these resources are located here:

http://www.scottlively.net/2014/08/19/not-just-another-sin/

Whether or not you choose to utilize these particular free resources or others that may be available on the Internet, it is essential that the church awaken to this threat and begin inoculating all Christian believers against "Gay Theology."

2. Repeal or Amend All Sexual Orientation Regulations and Restore the Right to Discriminate Against Homosexual Conduct

Second, we must redirect our focus against homosexuality itself and not secondary cultural battles. The Bible warns, and human experience confirms, that homosexuality is abnormal, unnatural and perverse conduct with severe personal and social consequences. It is not only appropriate, but necessary to social health and order to discriminate against homosexual conduct and ideology — even as we distinguish the person-hood of those who identify as homosexuals from their destructive lifestyle.

"Love the sinner, hate the sin," is a well-used and beautifully succinct summary of Christian theology on the matter, but somewhere along the way our movement got so focused on trying to show love for the sinner that we stopped reminding people why they should hate the sin. Probably because we got tricked into a posture of defensiveness by the "gay" movement's cynical tactic of equating all disagreement with their political agenda as hatred and fear of the "gays" themselves (thus the term "homophobia," which literally defines all disapproval of homosexuality as an anxiety disorder).

Not surprisingly, it was about that time in the American culture war when the pro-family side started losing the battles. Previously, when our campaigns exposed facts about homosexual practices, crimes, "gay" history, the relationship of homosexuality to pederasty, disease and mental illness, "hate-crime" hoaxes, and the corrupt conduct of "gay" leaders and activists, we won. When we started self-censoring those facts to try to prove we weren't "haters," we began to lose.

Recognizing our vulnerability, the "gays" began devoting themselves fully to pushing "anti-discrimination" policies defining "sexual orientation" as a basis for civil rights minority status. These Sexual Orientation Regulations (SORs) enshrine into law the logical premise that disapproval of homosexuality is morally wrong and must be publicly discouraged. They turn reality on its head and lead ultimately to the criminalization of Biblical Christianity. Moreover, wherever they have been enacted anywhere in the world, these SORs have proven to be the seed that contains the entire tree of the homosexual political agenda, with all of its poisonous fruit: "gay" marriage, "gay" adoption, indoctrination of public school children with "gay" propaganda, public funding of "gay" institutions, etcetera. Once the seed is planted, the entire agenda comes forth in steady incremental stages while dissent is increasingly punished.

It is this same flawed logical premise that allowed homosexuality to be granted the status of a "human right" in international law, one that increasingly now trumps the authentic human rights of religious freedom and natural family values.

In countries that have not yet adopted SORs, the pro-family movement should devote itself to preventing their enactment, and even passing prophylactic legislation recognizing the right of individuals, churches and businesses to favor natural family values and discriminate against homosexual conduct and ideology. Where SORs have already been enacted they must be repealed or amended to favor freedom of speech and religious liberty. I have drafted a model prophylactic statute for the American context, and a separate version of this model which may be used to amend existing SORs. Both may be adapted for use in other countries:

http://www.scottlively.net/2013/07/24/the-first-amendment-supremacy-clause-fact-sheet/

3. Persuade Family-Friendly Nations to Adopt the Russian Ban on Homosexual Propaganda to Children

Third, we need to build international pro-family solidarity on a foundation of genuine moral authority, meaning it must rest on the premise that homosexuality itself is personally and socially harmful, and not pretend that our only social and political interests are the "welfare of children" or the "definition of marriage." That pretense is a product of the same diseased pro-family "leadership" that marched the American pro-family movement from one disastrous defeat to the next for the past three decades, and it is now being exported to the rest of the world by the same men.

The beauty of the Russian law is it cuts right to the heart of the real problem of LGBT advocacy: the recruitment of children. What I mean by recruitment of children is not primarily the sexual exploitation of young people by adult homosexuals, though that represents a dark current within the larger "gay" culture, especially among the men. What I mean is the normalization of homosexual conduct and culture to children and youths, leading them to engage in homosexual experimentation among themselves and subsequently self-identify as "gay." An entire generation of American, British and Canadian children has been enslaved to this corrupt culture and ideology through the very propaganda that Russia has now banned.

While numerous countries of the African continent have chosen a much stricter approach, seeking to deter all homosexual conduct through harsh criminal sanctions, the Russian law balances the privacy rights of adult homosexuals (who choose to live discretely outside the mainstream of society) with the need of the nation to protect its children from the ravages of sexual perversion. It deters the LGBT lobby from attempting to mainstream the "gay" lifestyle, while granting the individual members of its community the "right to be left alone" that was the original stated goal of their movement in its early years, before it adopted the militant fascist tactics it is known for today.

I have been falsely accused of masterminding the Ugandan Anti-Homosexuality Bill which initially included the death penalty for repeat homosexual offenders, though I had strongly encouraged the Ugandan Parliament to emphasize rehabilitation and prevention, not punishment in my address to its members in 2009.

However, I am proud to say that I believe I played a small part in the adoption of the Russian law by advocating for such a policy in a 50-city speaking tour of Russia and the former Soviet Union in 2006 and 2007, ending in St. Petersburg where I published my Letter to the Russian People outlining my public policy recommendations. St. Petersburg became the first city to pass the law a couple of years later.

http://www.defendthefamily.com/pfrc/archives.php?id=5225300

My purpose in writing this Letter to the International Pro-Family Movement is to have a similar influence in the direction of public policy in other family-friendly nations.

I urge every pro-family advocate across the world to personally adopt the three simple goals outlined in this letter and to work toward their implementation. I further offer my services as a consultant, lecturer and/or strategist to assist pro-family advocacy groups around the world to achieve these goals.

Lastly, let us all pray that 2016 will be the year when the LGBT global campaign to homosexualize the world will finally be turned back.

###

THE (POTENTIALLY) BRIGHT FUTURE OF THE PRO-FAMILY MOVEMENT

Written July 20, 2017

What we call the pro-family movement is a component of the larger conservative movement and deals with matters of sexuality and the natural family. Its American roots are in the cultural backlash to the Marxist revolution of the 1960s that turned family-centered society on its head and swapped the Judeo-Christian morality of our founding for Soviet-style "political correctness."

Before the 1960s there wasn't any need for a "pro-family" movement because family values had been the overwhelming consensus of the western world for centuries. Indeed, so surprised were Americans about the cultural revolution that it took nearly twenty years for the conservatives to mount a truly effective response to it. That came under Ronald Reagan in the 1980s.

The 60's revolution was not grounded in the Marxist orthodoxy of Lenin and Stalin, but the Cultural Marxism of Herbert Marcuse's Frankfort School, which envisioned sexual anarchy, not a "workers revolt," as the key to dismantling Judeo-Christian civilization. The natural core constituency for this ideology was the underground "gay" movement whose dream of social acceptance was not possible without a complete transformation of American sexual morality. Thus, beginning in the late 1940s, Marxist organizer Harry Hay, so-called "father of the American gay movement" was also "father" of the (then hidden) army of "gay" activists most responsible for the "culture war" that exploded in the 60's and continues today.

America's Marxist revolution was therefore a "sexual revolution" whose overwhelming success vindicated Marcuse's destructive vision and became the primary tool of the one-world government elites for softening resistance to their domination by breaking the family-centered society which is every nation's greatest source of strength, stability and self-sufficiency.

Importantly, though primarily driven behind the scenes by "gays," the first goal was not legitimization of homosexual sodomy but the normalization of heterosexual promiscuity. This was the motive and strategy that drove "closeted" 1940s and 50s homosexual activist Alfred Kinsey's fraudulent "science" attacking the marriage-based sexual ethic as "repressive" and socially harmful. It also drove the launch of the modern porn industry, beginning with Hugh Hefner's *Playboy Magazine* (Hefner called himself "Kinsey's pamphleteer"). It drove and defined the battles in the courts where sexual morality was systematically "reformed" by Cultural Marxist elites on the US Supreme Court: contraception on demand to facilitate "fornication without consequences" (*Griswold v Connecticut* 1966), abortion on demand as the backup system to failed contraception (*Roe v Wade* 1973), and finally legalization of homosexual sodomy (*Lawrence v Texas* 2003).

Note the thirty year gap between *Roe v Wade* and *Lawrence v Texas*. That major delay in the Marxist agenda was achieved by the election of Ronald Reagan, under whom the pro-family movement became a major political force. That gap also highlights a critical fact: that "street activism" may be essential to any political cause but the real key to the culture war is the Supreme Court. By 1981 when Ronald Reagan took power the Marxists had nearly succeeded in collapsing the nation's family and economic infrastructure and the LGBT juggernaut had come completely out of the shadows and taken its place at the head of the cultural blitzkrieg it had been steering from the beginning. Reagan stopped that juggernaut by putting Antonin Scalia on the Supreme Court, the lion of constitutional originalism who wrote the majority opinion in *Bowers v Hardwick* (1986) which affirmed (not created) the constitutional right of states to criminalize homosexual sodomy and other harmful sexual conduct in the public interest.

Reagan and Scalia stopped the sexual revolution in its tracks and made it possible for the pro-family movement to begin restoring family values in society, which we strove diligently to do. I got my start in Christian social activism in those heady days and served as State Communications Director for the No Special Rights Act in Oregon in 1992 which forbade the granting of civil rights minority status based on sexual conduct. We fell short in Oregon but a Colorado version of our bill passed the same year. We had in essence won the culture war with that victory given that the Supreme Court had previously ruled that minority status designation required three things: a history of discrimination, political powerlessness, and immutable (unchangeable) status (such as skin color). We had a slam-dunk win on at least two of the three criteria and it would have been just a matter of time before we passed the No Special Rights law from coast to coast.

However, Reagan had been prevented by the elites from putting a second Scalia on the court in the person of Robert Bork, and was forced by the unprecedented political "borking" of Mr. Bork to accept their man Anthony Kennedy to fill the seat instead. Just ten years later, Kennedy served his function by writing the majority opinion killing the Colorado law in *Romer v Evans* (1996), audaciously declaring that the court didn't need to apply its three-part constitution test to the No Special Rights Act because it was motivated by "animus" (hate) and thus did not represent a legitimate exercise of the state's regulatory authority. The ruling was all the more outrageous given that it was only possibly through a blatant abuse of the court's own judicial authority. Kennedy's "disapproval = hate" lie set the tone for the political left from that point forward.

In *Lawrence v Texas*, Kennedy delivered the coup-de-grace to Justice Scalia by striking down *Bowers v Hardwick* and brazenly ruling that "public morality" cannot be the basis for law. Anthony Kennedy wrote the majority in all five SCOTUS opinions that have, in essence, established homosexual cultural supremacy in America, including the infamous and utterly unconstitutional *Obergefell v Hodges* (2015) "gay marriage" decision. He is, in my opinion, the worst and most culturally destructive jurist in the history of the court: the culprit (among many villainous candidates) most responsible for the current dysfunctional state of the family in America.

So where's the "bright future" amidst this lamentation? It's in the promise made and so-far kept by President Donald Trump to appoint only constitutional originalists to the supreme court. It is in the pleasantly surprising discovery that his first pick, Neil Gorsuch, seems from his first comments as a "supreme" to be a perfect choice to fill the "Scalia seat" on the court. It is in the hopeful rumors that Anthony Kennedy is about to retire, and the simple fact that ultra-hard leftist Ruth Bader Ginsberg and leftist Steven Broyer are of an age that their seats could at any time be vacated by voluntary or involuntary retirement.

In short, the bright future of the pro-family movement is in the hands of the man we hired to drain the swamp in Washington DC, and who hasn't yet backed down in that fight despite the remarkable scorched-earth campaign of destruction and discreditation being waged against him by the establishment elites of both parties, Hollywood and the media.

I must admit that after *Obergefell* I began to think that the pro-family movement had lost the culture war, but I now believe there is real hope, not just for reclaiming some lost ground, but possibly of reversing all of the "gains" of the hard left over the past half century. A solid majority of true constitutional originalists could actually restore the legal primacy of the natural family in America fairly quickly, and our cultural healing could quickly follow.

As the leftist elites and street activists continue their all-hands-on-deck attempted "borking" of President Trump, let's not forget why they're doing it. His political survival means the end of theirs. I can't think of a brighter future than that for our nation.

###

"GAY PRIDE" AND THE WRATH OF GOD

Written July 10, 2017

According to the third century Christian monks called the Desert Fathers, "pride" topped the list of the infamous Seven Deadly Sins. However, the Bible itself identifies homosexuality as the most deadly, giving it the special designation "*toeva*" (abomination) in the Leviticus 18 list of worst-possible sins which cause the land itself to "*vomit out*" its inhabitants, and making clear that widespread homosexuality was the cause of the incineration of Sodom and Gomorrah (Jude 1:7, referencing Genesis 19). That incident, unique in Biblical history, expressly linked male homosexual sodomy (and that sin alone) with the last-days destruction of the world by God.

So what should faithful Christians and Jews think of "Gay Pride," the international month-long celebration of homosexual sodomy that occurs every June, drawing support from numerous governments around the world?

The answer should be the clearest for the western nations with a Christian heritage, since the New Testament strongly reaffirms the condemnation of homosexuality found in the Old Testament. Romans 1:18-32 singularly identifies homosexuality as the sin that epitomizes the "*reprobate mind*" and the apostasy of the last days (see also 2 Timothy 3, Jude 1 and 2 Peter 2). Yet it is many of these "Christian" nations that are the most "affirming" of homosexual perversion. But Jewish Israel, especially Tel Aviv, is not far behind.

All cultures recognize that flags symbolize the powers that rule over a given territory. Raising its flag is the first action taken by any conquering power. How then should we interpret the raising of the rainbow flag across so many nations of the world, not just in June but whenever the "gay" movement is formally acknowledged? For example, on the US Supreme Court's issuance of the *Obergefell* "gay marriage" ruling, Barack Obama used colored lights to bath the White House in a rainbow flag. Importantly, no other special interest group receives such honor by the ruling authorities. Spiritually-minded people should recognize this as a phenomenon with deep significance.

Just what does the rainbow itself symbolize and why do the "gays" cloak themselves in it?

The rainbow is the Biblical symbol of the presence and authority of God from the story of Noah's Flood, foundational to all the Abrahamic faiths, reaffirmed to Jews and Christians in Ezekiel 1:28, and to Christians in Revelation 4:3 in the New Testament. Could there be any more audacious statement of defiance of God than to hijack His symbol to represent the worldwide legitimization of sexual deviance He explicitly condemns? Could this be the meaning of the prophecy of the Antichrist in Revelation 6:2?: "*I looked, and there before me was a white horse! Its rider held a bow, and he was given a crown, and he rode out as a conqueror bent on conquest.*"

Does this verse definitively associate the "gay" movement with the Antichrist of the last days? No. Neither does the spiritual comparison of Jerusalem with "*Sodom and Egypt*" under the Antichrist in Revelation 11:8. Nor do modern "gay rights" laws that require Christian businesses such as bakers, printers and florists to endorse homosexuality – so reminiscent of restrictions on "buying and selling" imposed on those refusing to take the "Mark of the Beast" (Revelation 13:17). Still, it should give every Christian pause that the Bible's many warnings about homosexuality from Genesis to Revelation are tied so closely to the last days and to extreme rebellion triggering God's wrath, especially when these passages are viewed collectively.

Indeed, the ancient prophecy of Isaiah contains the following verse that seems so timely today:

"The expression of their faces bears witness against them, And they display their sin like Sodom; They do not even conceal it. Woe to them! For they have brought evil on themselves" (Isaiah 3:9).

This appears a perfect caption for the scene at "Gay Pride" parades, and invokes the many horrors that afflict the "gay" community: from a long string of gruesome "gay on gay" slayings, such as the Jeffrey Dahmer cannibal killings, and murders of Matthew Shepard and Giani Versace, to the lingering movement-wide plague of AIDS and other frightening STDs (carefully minimized by the pro-"gay" press).

The current "gay" supremacist version of the LGBT movement was born June 28th, 1969 in the notorious Stonewall Riots, when homosexual men violently attacked police officers seeking to arrest a boy "drag queen" prostitute at the Mafia-owned Stonewall Bar on Christopher Street in New York City. That was the origin of "Gay Pride Day," and of the vicious, implacable army of "gay" activists who have battled ever since to transform every institution of western society into a tool of LGBT advocacy. Since that day, any person who opposes them in any meaningful way faces an intense campaign of personal destruction. By these means they have nearly achieved the end of the family-centered order of civilization my generation took for granted just a a half-century ago.

The Apostle Peter wrote only two short letters in the Bible. The second of these is devoted to prophecy about the last days, and it's special emphasis was to warn the church about a form of heresy that would then emerge. In Christianity, heresy is a set of beliefs that contradict the clear teaching of the Bible. According to Peter, the last days heresy will be rooted in beliefs about sexuality "*Many will follow their sensuality, and because of them the way of the truth will be maligned,*" he wrote in 2 Peter 2:2. He went on to define this heresy by reference to four Biblical texts addressing sexual sin, including especially homosexuality. A close reading of 2 Peter 2 strongly suggests that the last days heresy is so-called "gay theology."

Christians should not be surprised that the world today, and the US especially, is in such a mess. We've been steadily losing the "culture war" that in so many ways is a contest pitting LGBT values against ours. And if these are the last days, that's the way things are supposed to be. However, our responsibility to stand steadfastly for truth has never changed and is not contingent on circumstances.

We must always "*contend earnestly for the faith entrusted once for all to the saints*" (Jude 1:3). That means having the courage to speak the truth ourselves, to work vigorously to purge the heresy of "gay theology" from the church, and to continue to fight the culture war to win it, trusting God for whatever outcome will result. Lastly, we must rescue as many souls as we can from the seductive evil of "Gay Pride," knowing that the wrath it heralds is too terrible to wish upon even our worst enemies.

###

'GAY' RECOVERY, RECIDIVISM AND GRACE

Published September 5, 2017

Ex-"gays" have been a part of the Christian church from its earliest days. After reminding believers that "*homosexuals*" and "*effeminates*" (male transsexuals) "*will not inherit the Kingdom of God,*" the Apostle Paul wrote: "*And such were some of you: but ye are washed, but ye are sanctified, but ye are justified in the name of the Lord Jesus, and by the Spirit of our God*" (1 Corinthians 6:9-11).

This scripture was foundational to the ministry of Exodus International, which served as a hub for many independent groups of ex-"gays" around the world from 1976 to 2013. Exodus was so named to evoke the exodus of the Hebrew slaves from Egypt in the Bible, and to analogize compulsive same-sex attraction and conduct to slavery from which one could be delivered by God.

Though I have never experienced same-sex attraction, I attended several Exodus conferences and other functions and was deeply impressed by the glowing Christian character of many of its members and the overpowering presence of the Holy Spirit, especially during their worship in music. I have always had a special place in my heart for "gay" strugglers and have ministered to many individuals over the years as an aspect of my Bible-based Christian activism.

As with any compulsive behavioral disorder, homosexuality is tough to overcome. There's an aspect of physiology involved in all addictions – drugs, alcohol, food, gambling, video games, porn, whatever – that addicts the struggler to his or her own pleasure-related brain chemicals that are released when they act out. Unlike most other addictions, however, sex-based ones are especially hard to escape because sexuality is hard-wired in us and the brain chemistry associated with sexual release is extraordinarily powerful. If you never experienced cocaine, you'd never miss it, but everyone is sexual by nature, and the sexual impulse is continual throughout life, whether you want it or not.

Once your brain associates sexual pleasure with any particular illicit act or fetish – especially during the formative years – the stage is set for possible addiction. You can't un-ring the bell and you can't prevent the bell from ringing again in the part of your brain where temptations dwell. The more you indulge the temptation, the louder and more insistent the bell will ring. What is worse, the shame associated with indulgence create an inner turmoil which enhances the effect of the brain chemistry and becomes a part of the addictive cycle.

I was miraculously healed of drug and alcohol addiction in 1986 – on my knees in prayer at a treatment center – after sixteen years of bondage that started at the age of 12. I never had another desire to drink or take drugs ever again. Nevertheless, I attended Alcoholics Anonymous regularly for over a year and saw that for many addicts temptation fades very slowly but they can stay abstinent through the constant mutual encouragement of fellow-sufferers. A few years later when I became familiar with Exodus International, I noticed that the successful local groups of ex-"gays" seemed to follow the same general approach.

AA enjoys enormous public support, even among drunks who don't wish to seek recovery. Nevertheless, the recidivism rate for alcoholics is very high. Exodus International, on the other hand, suffered the wrath of the powerful LGBT political movement from Day One because every one of its members was living proof that homosexual self-indulgence is a choice. Every member was thus individually a target – with the goal of forcing them to recant and re-commit to a "gay" self-identification. And, of course, many did, including Alan Chambers, who closed Exodus in 2013 with an apology for ever suggesting homosexuals could overcome same-sex temptation.

Alan went back to Egypt, metaphorically speaking, while the network of ex-"gay" groups simply migrated from Exodus to the more Biblically-oriented Restored Hope Network and added him to their prayer list.

But if vilification and ridicule are the "stick," then the "carrot" in "gay" recidivism is so-called "gay theology:" the Christian heresy that fraudulently reinterprets the Bible to change its message from condemnation to affirmation of homosexuality. From apostate Derrick Sherwin Bailey's *Homosexuality and the Western Christian Tradition* in 1955 to the just-published manifesto "The Statement" http://www.christiansunitedstatement.org/ (in response to the Biblically grounded "Nashville Statement" on LGBT issues https://cbmw.org/nashville-statement/), "gay theology" has always been satanic bait to lure those with same-sex attraction into lives of active homosexual sin. It is also a seductive siren-song for ex-"gays" in the weak moments of their recovery.

In tandem with "gay theology" is the heresy of antinomianism, which holds that salvation by grace frees the Christian believer from accountability to the moral law (which fails the most basic test of logic if theft or murder is substituted for sodomy in the equation: *reductio-ad-absurdum*). Antinomianism is the heresy Paul debunked in the book of Romans, which, importantly, begins with a correlation of homosexuality with the "reprobate mind" (Rom 1:18-32), before launching into a detailed treatise on law and grace in chapters 2-8, contrasting "justification" (salvation by faith alone, Rom 5:1), with "sanctification" (becoming Christlike, Rom 6:12-19).

Effective ministry to Christian "ex-"gays" and backsliders requires a basic understanding of Paul's teaching. While justification is by faith alone, sanctification requires work: specifically, following the spirit of the moral law that underlies the letter of the law proactively. To the argument that "gay sex" (or stealing) will send you to hell, the heretics cite "salvation by faith alone" and they're right on that narrow technicality when taken out of context.

But their deadly error is missing the truth about sanctification: 1) becoming Christlike is not possible without following the spirit of the moral law and cooperating with Him in the transformation process, and 2) only a false Christ contradicts the spirit of the moral law to rationalize sin, meaning if you're doing that in His name you're probably not saved because you can't be justified by faith in a false Christ. This is why *"faith without works is dead"* (James 2:20) because faith is proved by its fruit (changed character and behavior) – as measured by the spirit of the moral law.

"Gay" heresy also confuses grace with mercy. Grace is God's dispensation of an unearned gift, while mercy is His forgiveness for sin-earned punishment. Moral equations involving homosexuality and its consequences are not governed by grace but mercy. Thus, the darkest spiritual condition arises from declaring that homosexual temptation and conduct is a "gift" of God (blaspheming Him – and the Holy Spirit – by contradicting His explicit moral law), while simultaneously pushing away His hand of mercy by insisting that homosexual sin doesn't need forgiveness. Such a person is doubly cursed.

"Gay theology" is thus not just a threat to the integrity of the Church, it is a diabolical trap designed to ensnare same-sex attracted believers in a soul-binding heresy. Our duty is to boldly affirm the truth and encourage them to do the same – especially if they're backslidden – because grace can come only from the true Christ, and forgiveness is only effective for those who admit they need it.

The Apostle John perhaps said it best in 1 John 1:8-10: *"If we say that we have no sin, we deceive ourselves, and the truth is not in us. If we confess our sins, he is faithful and just to forgive us our sins, and to cleanse us from all unrighteousness. If we say that we have not sinned, we make him a liar, and his word is not in us."* That graceful summary contains both the essence of "gay" recovery and the remedy for recidivism.

###

Endnotes

[1] The Book of Hosea is especially instructive to this teaching, as the two "Houses" of the divided Hebrew kingdom, Judea and Israel, are portrayed as wives of God, condemned as adulterers for worship of false gods.

[2] Massachusetts General Laws, Chapter 272, Crimes Against Chastity, Morality, Decency and Good Order, Section 34, Crime against nature: "Whoever commits the abominable and detestable crime against nature, either with mankind or with a beast, shall be punished by imprisonment in the state prison for not more than twenty years."

[3] Paragraph 25. H. 8. C. 6. Buggery is twofold. 1. With mankind, 2. With beasts. Buggery is the Genus, of which Sodomy and Bestiality, are the species. 12. Co. 37. Says, "note that Sodomy is with mankind." But Finch's L. B. 3. c. 24. "Sodomiary is a carnal copulation against nature, to wit, of man or woman in the same sex, or of either of them with beasts." 12. Co. 36. Says, "it appears by the ancient authorities of the law that this was felony." Yet the 25. H. 8. Declares it felony, as if supposed not the be so.... B. Fleta, L. i. c. 37. says, "pecorantes et Sodomitae in terra vivi confodiantur." The Mirror makes it treason. Bestiality can never make any progress; it cannot therefore be injurious to society in any great degree, which is the true measure of criminality in foro civili, and will ever be properly and severely punished, by universal derision. It may, therefore, be omitted. It was anciently punished with death, as it has been latterly. Ll. Aelfrid. 31. and 25. H. 8. c. 6. see Beccaria. Paragraph 31. Montesq." Peterson, Merrill D. "Crimes and Punishments" Thomas Jefferson: Writings Public Papers (Literary Classics of the United States, Inc. 1984) pp. 355, 356.

[4] In *Call of the Torah,* Rabbi Elie Munk interprets the sin against Noah as "an act of pederasty" (p. 220).

[5] In my view, the "religion" of the Antichrist will not be one of the established religions or some new phenomenon, it will be simply U.S. and U.N.-style Secular Humanism, enforced by an all-powerful dictator who demands worship as a God among men: a modern version of the human-led polytheism that Antiochus Epiphanes, the Pharaohs of Eqypt and the Emperors of Rome imposed on their subjects.

[6] A useful resource for investigating the so-called "Two House Teaching" is www.jewsandjoes.com.

THE PETROS PROPHECY: SIMON PETER'S WARNING ABOUT THE HERESY OF THE LAST DAYS

ABOUT THE AUTHOR

Dr. Scott Lively is a one of the world's foremost experts on the so-called culture war as it relates to the global homosexual movement and agenda and has served as an advocate for the Biblical world-view on these issues for over a quarter century, with service in more than 50 countries.

A Christian attorney with litigation experience in US Constitutional Law, he holds the degree of *Juris Doctor* (*magna cum laude*) from Trinity Law School. He earned a Doctorate of Theology from the Pentecostal Assemblies of God. His doctoral thesis has been published in book form under the title *Redeeming the Rainbow: A Christian Response to the 'Gay' Agenda*. He also holds a Bachelor of Science Degree in Management and Communication from Western Baptist College, and a Certificate in International Human Rights from the Institute for Human Rights at the University of Strasbourg (France).

Dr. Lively and his wife Anne have been married for 35 years, have four sons and seven grandchildren. Their home base is Springfield, Massachusetts where they founded an inner city mission in 2008 to serve the disadvantaged, but most of their time is spent in travel as Missionaries to the Global Pro-Family Movement.

THE PETROS PROPHECY: SIMON PETER'S WARNING ABOUT THE HERESY OF THE LAST DAYS

www.ingramcontent.com/pod-product-compliance
Lightning Source LLC
Chambersburg PA
CBHW071707040426
42446CB00011B/1949